THE
MENAGERIE
MEMOIRS

A Tryst with
Wildlife at Home

THE MENAGERIE MEMOIRS

A Tryst with Wildlife at Home

SHASHIDHAR M K

Notion Press

Old No. 38, New No. 6

McNichols Road, Chetpet

Chennai - 600 031

First Published by Notion Press 2016

Copyright © Shashidhar M K 2016

All Rights Reserved.

ISBN 978-93-5206-744-2

Dedicated to

(Parents)
Late Smt. Janaki Iengar and Late Sri. M K S Iengar

(Brother)
Late Sri. M K Srinath

CONTENTS

FOREWORD

I was quite surprised when my good friend requested me to write the foreword for his forthcoming book. I know very little about animals and animal rehabilitation. My only qualification was that I know Dr Shashidhar and his family and their work for four decades. I wonder if this is good enough.

I consider it my privilege to write this foreword. Dr Shashidhar and his family have been doing yeoman service in the field of animal rescue and welfare through the trust they have formed – Animal Rescue and Rehabilitation Trust (ARRT). The dedication of the whole family to this work is to be seen to be believed. Since many years, even as young medical students, we have been visiting their house that was better known as the 'Mini Zoo.' The loving care Shashidhar's parents gave these animals in need of help, was phenomenal. It was remarkable to see the whole family give time and effort for this cause. The enthusiasm was so contagious that any new entrant to the family would soon be actively participating in these activities.

What is very impressive is the time spent by ARRT on documenting events and educating the lay public. Sheeba was, of course, a star. The loving care she got made sure that she survived – a little miracle in itself. As Shashidhar says in the book, nature had decided that she was not fit for survival. The attention she got was important in that it drew the attention of the media and the public to the great work being done by ARRT. Myths, folklore and the wrong impression we all have about snakes are well known. Dr Shashidhar (and his late brother in the past) has given several presentations in schools, colleges and clubs demystifying snakes and spreading rational, scientific facts. This work by itself deserves high praise.

This book gives a little peek into the kind of work ARRT has been doing. It gives lay persons like us a little taste of what life is among animals – highlighting the events surrounding the lioness Sheeba, in the first part and snakes and other animals in the latter part. The flow is easy; language is simple. The genuine interest shown in rehabilitation and the simple innovations needed to support these animals in need, come across very clearly in the book.

I congratulate Dr Shashidhar and his family on the excellent work they have done in the field of animal rehabilitation and wish this book every 'success' – it is a source of great learning for all of us.

Dr K Lakshman

FRCS

Consultant Surgeon

ACKNOWLEDGEMENT

- Forest Department of Karnataka
- Karuna Animal Shelter, Bangalore
- Animal Welfare Board of India
- The Born Free Foundation, United Kingdom
- My wife Sharada and my daughter Shruthi
- The Media and all the well-wishers of the Animal Rescue and Rehabilitation Trust (ARRT)

SHEEBA—QUEEN OF THE JUNGLE

Not even in my wildest dreams had I imagined that I would be spending a year or so with the Queen of the Jungle. Of course, when she came into our lives, she was a Princess and not yet a Queen. She was helpless. She was a tawny brown ball of soft fur with big black eyes. She was quite timid. Naturally, in a strange environment, anybody would feel out of place – even if she were to be a princess. Yes, I am talking about a lioness cub which came into our lives and enlivened and enlightened us during her stay with us for a year.

How did the princess come into this predicament? Well, there is a prelude to the story, or rather, facts.

THE PRELUDE: Sheeba, the small little brown ball of fur that I call Princess, was born on February 6, 1996, with two more cubs. The mother lioness did not try to feed the three cubs. Two siblings of Sheeba died in a matter of a few weeks, because of the lack of maternal care. The authorities concerned could have forestalled the tragedy with timely intervention. But, fate willed it this way. Fortunately, for the third cub, there was a miracle waiting to happen.

We had been to Bannerghatta National Park to see how Piggy, our wild boar which was rehabilitated from ARRT, was getting along. After feeding Piggy some biscuits, which she was used to eating while at our residence, we were planning to return home. At that time, somebody in the park mentioned that there was a lion cub at the Veterinary Doctor's office. It was neglected by its mother. We wanted to see how a lion cub would be. We were expecting to see a cuddly, robust, energetic ball of fur. The sight that met our eyes was a pathetic one. The lion cub reminded us of the children in Ethiopia – malnourished with a bloated belly and thin limbs. There was a big bald patch of skin on its forehead where it was brushing against the metal enclosure constantly, before it was shifted to its present location in the Veterinarian's Office.

The cub was dehydrated and looked sick. She had a bout of diarrhoea which further dehydrated her. The caretaker of this patient was a small boy, who hardly understood the gravity of the situation and the crisis at hand. He looked very casual with all the other loose motions of the lion cub around him in the room. On asking, the boy told us that the Vet was on leave for a few days, and there was no replacement for him. We immediately took stock of the situation. I had seen how bouts of loose motions can cause severe dehydration and weakness among fit young adults.

The lion cub was in such a pitiable state with no one to care for her. We asked the Deputy Conservator of Forests whether he would permit us to nurse the cub at ARRT, and return it to the park once it recovered. We explained to the officer that the situation was like having a hospital with in-patients but without any personnel to look after the patients after office hours. The patients were at the mercy of the elements once the office staff left at the end of the day. The officer knew all about the various animals that we had rescued at ARRT and rehabilitated, and the good work that we had carried out over the past thirty years or so. In no time, the officer gave his consent and the lion cub was on its way to ARRT and a bright future.

This was Sheeba at three months, weighing a mere three kilos when she made an entry to ARRT at the end of May 1996.

While driving back home over a distance of about twenty kilometres, Sheeba had a couple of bouts of loose motions. It made us wonder whether our bold move to get her to ARRT was correct or not.

The moment we saw Sheeba at the park, we made a diagnosis. Sheeba had too much cow's milk without any solids, such as minced meat and the like. The condition was something like lactose intolerance. It was like a one-year-old human child, continuing to be on a milk diet without any solids. Naturally, the child is undernourished. With the amount of milk being given to sustain its health, there was bound to be intolerance. This was the case with Sheeba. Continuous loose motions can sap anybody's strength and Sheeba, being a very small animal with no medical support, suffered the consequences. The first step was to stop feeding her milk. Minced meat was given next. For the first time in her life, Sheeba had access to solid food. The very next day, the loose motions stopped and Sheeba was on her way to recovery. All of us heaved a sigh of relief. The worst was over! The rough bare patch on her forehead was due to constant rubbing against the iron bars of the enclosure. This gradually disappeared. There was also the unhealthy look and loss of skin turgor. These things were set right over a period of a few weeks.

But, we had a problem, in that we did not know how much meat a lion cub of this age would eat. The problem was not as bad as it seemed. Unlike human beings, who continue to overeat even after their hunger is appeased, animals do not overeat and if offered food when they are not hungry, they simply ignore it.

There are many behavioural peculiarities which we observed on the first day itself. Many of us who have had cats for pets may have observed that if they are not allowed access to relieve themselves and are confined to a small place, they look out for a normal drainage area to relieve themselves. The same thing happened on the first day. We were wondering how to make Sheeba comfortable. While we were busy discussing, we did not pay attention to Sheeba's disappearing act. One of us heard the sound of water trickling in the bathroom and thought it must have been because of a faulty tap. When we entered the bathroom, we were surprised to see Sheeba adjusting her huge body, just to focus on the sieve of the bathroom, so that all her urine would pass close to the sieve. We were surprised! All cats, irrespective of their size, and status as domestic or wild creatures, follow this routine to keep their habitat clean.

Sheeba was quite disturbed, nervous and edgy because of her new surroundings. The lack of maternal care, which was required at this phase of its life, added to the problem. This was evident from the restlessness she showed. Suddenly, I thought of the method children use to pacify themselves by sucking their thumbs. Sheeba would have fallen asleep while suckling at her mother's teats. So, I just put my thumb into her mouth, and sure enough, she started sucking strongly on my thumb. She had baby teeth which were quite sharp, but she would not bite on my thumb - just like how she would not have harmed her mother's teats. This sucking business went

Young sheeba sucking thumb

on for quite a few weeks starting from the first day. In the night, as we were preparing to go to bed, we would put Sheeba with us on the mattress. My daughter, who was about nine years old at that time, would be sharing the bed with her parents. Sheeba would put her head on my shoulder or chest, and, depending on which side she would sleep on, I would put the appropriate thumb into her mouth. She would keep sucking on my thumb for quite some time. I would go off to sleep with my thumb inside Sheeba's mouth. One thing to be noted here is that the tongue of all carnivores is very rough. It is like a rasp. This is to enable them to pick up the last bits of flesh sticking to the bone. The effect of this thumb-sucking, even though it lulled Sheeba to sleep, was the downside - a sore thumb for me! Even though there was no blood-letting at any time, the powerful suction and the simultaneous tongue movement left the skin of my thumb quite sore. But it was a small price to pay for the contentment on the little cub's face. She would have probably been dreaming of her mother and imagining her feeding the young.

On the whole, the first half day was remarkable and absorbing for all of us. Who would imagine, that one day, a lioness would be strutting around in our house, having free access to all the places - including our bedrooms and bathrooms?

Sheeba slept peacefully amidst the three of us the whole night. Our warmth was very much needed for her to be comfortable through the night.

The next morning saw the family waking up as usual. We had to pay attention to Sheeba's requirements. First of all, we made it to the compound and the garden for her to relieve herself. We had a Tulsi plant in the corner with a few bricks isolating it from the rest of the garden. Sheeba took a fancy to it and made it her loo till the end of her stay with us. A lot of wet mud in the garden and the solid food eaten for the first time worked itself up to give a strong bowel movement. The poop was quite solid without an iota of liquid element in it. We were happy that the bowel movement was normal. Maybe this was the first time anybody would be so happy seeing an animal's poop. Since there was not much free mud to cover it, Sheeba made a few instinctive scraping movements mimicking covering of her excreta.

Sheeba fell into a routine in the following days. We wanted her to be independent and sleep on her own at night. We made a place for her in the living room. We brought a dog collar and a chain to restrict her movements during certain hours of the day. She would be tied up to the leg of the library shelf from where she could see us and we would be able to keep an eye on her. A round-shaped four-feet-diameter carpet was made her exclusive property. She would play with the edge of the carpet, go under it and sleep on it.

Whenever Sheeba had the urge to relieve herself during her "chained" moments, she would clearly indicate her intentions by standing up in her place and staring at us. No sound escaped her throat. In fact, throughout her stay with us she never once growled or whined. Maybe this was because she had never heard the sounds made by any member of her pride.

As Sheeba became accustomed to her new surroundings, and with the amount of love and affection shown to her by all the family members, and also the visitors who thronged our residence to have a glimpse of the would-be "Queen of the Jungle," Sheeba slowly started playing her own tricks on us. She had her own game plans. The most popular game for Sheeba was 'Hide and Seek.' The first time Sheeba started the game, she took us by surprise. It was really dangerous if one was not anticipating the sudden rush of her tawny body and the impact it would have on us. To be fair to Sheeba, she was always thinking that we were one of her own kind and played accordingly. You would have observed how kittens play among themselves. One of the kittens would behind the pots in the garden and keep a watch on the others. When the others were not watching and tending to themselves, the kitten in hiding would rush out all of a sudden and pounce on the other siblings. The sibling would be equally agile and take the sudden attack in its stride and both would go somersaulting without anyone getting injured.

Now imagine this situation – You are standing alone without knowing that a huge muscular body weighing around thirty kilograms was hiding in the bushes in your own garden. Then, there would be a hazy blur of a tawny body rushing towards you at full throttle and pouncing on you. Unless you had braced yourself for this attack, you would be off-balance in no time and sent sprawling across with disastrous consequences. Since this game of hide and seek started when Sheeba was young and weighing only a few kilograms, we got used to being careful and watching Sheeba's moves in advance. This has saved us from visiting an Orthopaedician many a times.

Another game was to run behind us and try to catch us by hitting out with her front paws, which were huge. Maybe Sheeba was practicing her hunting skills imagining one of us to be an antelope.

Sheeba growing up

Once we got used to her games, we wanted to know what Sheeba would do if we allowed her to catch us. When she was very young she would rise up on her hind legs and catch us at the height of our thigh, grip it with her front paws and give a mock bite without injuring us. But, as she grew older, the impact was such that there would be small bruises, despite the bite being harmless.

Sheeba's eating habits were excellent. As Sheeba was growing bigger by the day, we had to increase the amount of chopped meat every week. After a few weeks, we started giving her small bits of bone mixed with the meat. Often, Sheeba would swallow the bone piece whole. Sheeba, who was skinny and would have passed for a malnourished big breed of dog, was now very plump, healthy and full of energy.

A few abnormalities of Sheeba's became evident as she grew up. Despite good nutrition, we saw that there was a problem in her hind limbs. Both the hip joints were weak. This, we could gauge and say with certainty, because Sheeba was always reluctant to stand when she was sitting on her haunches and would prefer to be standing rather than sit. This we started observing at an early age, even though walking and running was not affected at all. We assumed it to be a congenital hip anomaly on both sides.

Another deformity we noticed was that the front paws of both sides were rotated inwards at an angle. After observing a normal lion this problem was noticed in Sheeba.

The vision in her left eye was also suspect. This was evident because she was liable to bump into objects on her left side. This was proved by waving one's hand on hers left side and noting that there was no response.

On close examination it was evident that there was a cataract developing in the left eye and also the cornea and eyeball were more protruding and tense on the left side. Was there an increase in intraocular pressure, perhaps, glaucoma?

It now dawned on us now that these abnormalities would have made her unfit to survive in the wild. It was Charles Darwin's "Survival of the

Fittest" at work. These abnormalities took some time to be noticed by us, whereas Sheeba's mother had already passed the verdict as soon as she was born. Her maternal instinct had told her that this cub would not pass muster and hence the best thing would be to abandon the offspring by neglecting it. What a waste of time and effort for a cub to be nurtured to adulthood when it would not stand a chance in the wild, competing with normal brethren. Nature in the wild sees to it that most of the abnormal offspring of any animal except that of humans would not make it to adulthood. This would avoid propagation of congenital anomalies further in their pride or herd as the case may be.

The question now arises as to why Sheeba was born with these defects. The answer is 'inbreeding.' As everyone knows, consanguineous marriages are frowned upon among humans. Many of us have seen or read about these "close relationship" marriages causing the recessive chromosomes to come out in the open without the dominant chromosomes present in both partners, to protect this outcome of characteristics.

The lions in the park had the same problem. Every lion and lioness was related to each other very closely – as close as say – father-daughter, mother-son, grandfather-granddaughter and so on. Cousins and nephews were aplenty. There was no segregation of the female in oestrous and nobody would know who had fathered whose offspring. Added to this, there were African species and Indian species freely mingling with each other. Hence, there was no surprise that Sheeba was born with these anomalies.

Anyway, these problems would not come in the way of her daily routine except the vision in the left eye.

One day, maybe about three weeks after Sheeba's arrival, my daughter Shruthi, after coming back from school in the evening, noticed a change in the cub's behaviour. She told us that there was anger on Sheeba's face as she was snarling. We had not observed anything wrong at the time of feeding, Sheeba with meat and bones. Sure enough, my daughter's observation was true. Indeed, she was making an expression of discomfort and was trying to put a paw into her mouth as though trying to take out something that stuck inside. I tried to pacify Sheeba and told her in a comforting tone that I was there to help her.

People with pet dogs swear that dogs can follow their thought even if they do not vocalize it. This is true among wild animals including our Sheeba. I boldly put my hand inside Sheeba's mouth and felt whether there was anything troubling Sheeba. The way she was behaving prompted me to feel the palate of her mouth. The upper part of the mouth of all carnivores is ridged and not smooth. When I felt Sheeba's palate it was smooth. I could not make out any bone stuck there. Then, I felt her palate deeper in the mouth. I could feel that there was a hard piece of bone jutting behind into her mouth. This bone piece was rectangular in shape and the size was such that it had gotten wedged perfectly between the two rows of teeth of the upper jaw, flush with the palate. No way could it be dislodged and Sheeba was trying to put her paw into the mouth, showing discomfort at the same time. Once, I had concluded that there was a bone piece tightly stuck, I had to manually remove it. I told my daughter to get ready with the video camera and choose the correct angle to shoot the 'operation' of bone removal. This was indeed an opportunity of a lifetime to put one's hand into the mouth of a lion and remove a foreign body without any sedation to the lioness.

Full marks to Sheeba for the excellent cooperation. Soothing words, gentle movements, no panic, and no fear among the participants saw the whole drama conclude in a matter of minutes. I put my hand along the palate of Sheeba and felt the ridge of the protruding bone. I just yanked it out of the palate in a swift movement. Sheeba was immediately relieved of her distress and we had an amateur recording of the proceedings. Sheeba was curious to know the cause of her misery. I let her smell the bone piece and gave it to her to munch on. There was no injury to Sheeba's mouth and the whole episode ended on a happy note.

Sheeba would play with a big plastic ball – the size of a football, in the compound. She would just push the ball with her feet and run behind it. Unlike a dog, she was not too keen on continuing the game. When we substituted the big plastic ball with a soft tennis ball there was a transformation in her attitude. The softness of the ball made her hold on to it in her mouth as if it was some prey. She would not let go of the ball and there was an element of anger. For the first time we felt a little insecure. We had to induce her to drop the ball by offering juicy steaks of meat. That was the last time we gave her a soft toy to play with.

In the evenings, we used to sit outside in the compound near the gate. We would tie Sheeba to the gate like a dog. She loved the atmosphere there. She would watch people walking up and down the road, vehicles moving, children playing on the streets and so on. Every evening, Sheeba would wait for the clock to strike five because that was the time she would enjoy the open air. She would be brought in at dusk.

After a month or so, Sheeba was growing rapidly. Every week we would increase the quantity of meat by about a quarter kilogram and watch her gobble up the full amount.

We had to find a place for Sheeba to sleep at night as we could not accommodate her on our mattress anymore. We managed to put her in one of the attached bathrooms. For a few

Relieving herself

days, she welcomed the new resting place. But, as time passed by she got bored to sleep in isolation and in a confined place. That was the time we decided to secure her to the wooden leg of the library shelf, in the drawing room. Except for the night lamp, all other lights would be switched off. This was well tolerated by Sheeba and she did not make any fuss or show resentment.

I had earlier narrated how Sheeba had chosen one particular spot in the garden as her restroom. Initially, we had thought that the high urea content in her urine (because of meat diet) would aid the growth of plants. But, over a few weeks we could see that there was so much fertiliser content in the urine that the leaves of the plants were burning out and dying slowly. In a couple of months, the plants in that area gradually died out.

During the first month of her stay, Sheeba was unable to scale the compound wall which was of three feet height. It was pretty safe to leave her free in the compound. As Sheeba grew in size, we realised that it was a matter of few weeks before she would attempt to explore the streets and neighbourhood on her own. We decided to put up a grill over the compound wall to contain Sheeba and avoid any mishaps either to her or the public at large. The house resembled a fortress now. The exterior of the house was built of stone blocks and the added grill work completed the picture of a fortress.

One day in the evening, Sheeba was, as usual, enjoying herself at the gate of the house. She was restrained with a collar and chain. One of my friends happened to visit me. Since I was at the gate, he greeted me. He opened the gate himself and entered the compound. We made ourselves comfortable in the living room. As we were discussing something, my friend suddenly asked which breed the dog at the gate was. I casually told him that it was a lioness and not a dog. My friend thought that I was joking and trying to pull his leg. He asked me to be serious. I said I was dead serious and she was indeed a lioness. My friend was not convinced. He said no matter what other animals we had at home - whether snakes, owls, kites, mongoose or anything else - this was going to the extreme. I assured him again that she was a lioness. Then, I asked him to accompany me to the gate and see for himself. As he approached Sheeba, the truth dawned on him slowly. He looked at Sheeba's face and realised how massive she was. No dog in the world had a face so huge. Then, I asked him to look at the paws. They were at least three times the size of a dog's. And the muscles! What muscles in the chest and forelimbs? Looking at these features, my friend suddenly lost his nerve and became scared. He told me to hold the animal back so that he could make a quick exit. I reminded him of how fearlessly he had walked in a few minutes ago. He told that he had not realised it was a lion, and mistaking it for a dog, had casually walked in. This way, ignorance is bliss. As I held Sheeba back, my friend made a dash through the open gates to his vehicle and was off in a trice. He called out from a distance to say goodbye.

As Sheeba grew up, we expected the milk teeth to fall off and expected a gap in the dentition like human children. We never noticed the transition from milk teeth to adult dentition. Sheeba was able to crunch on fairly big bones and digest them as well.

Sheeba required a bath every week. There would be three or four of us to help in the process. Usually, the bath would be given in the forenoon period. The garden hose was very handy for this. We had some human usage shampoo bottle. A 100 ml bottle of shampoo would last for a single bath. Initially, the water from the hose was used to wet the hair all over and allow it to penetrate to the skin. The initial spurt of water was not well received by Sheeba. But once the process started, she loved the bath. I would rub the Shampoo into her entire body. It was a really tiring process. When Sheeba was young, the surface area was small and it was not so tiring. But when Sheeba was six or seven months old, it was quite taxing. Care had to be taken to not get the water or shampoo in her ear. Removing the shampoo required a lot of water since it would have gotten into the deeper layers of the fur. We would then let Sheeba get rid of the excess water by shaking herself vigorously. Drying up the hair with a big thick towel was the next step. Sheeba would then be tied to the gate to sunbathe and dry herself. This whole process would have taken a couple of hours and we would ourselves need a bath.

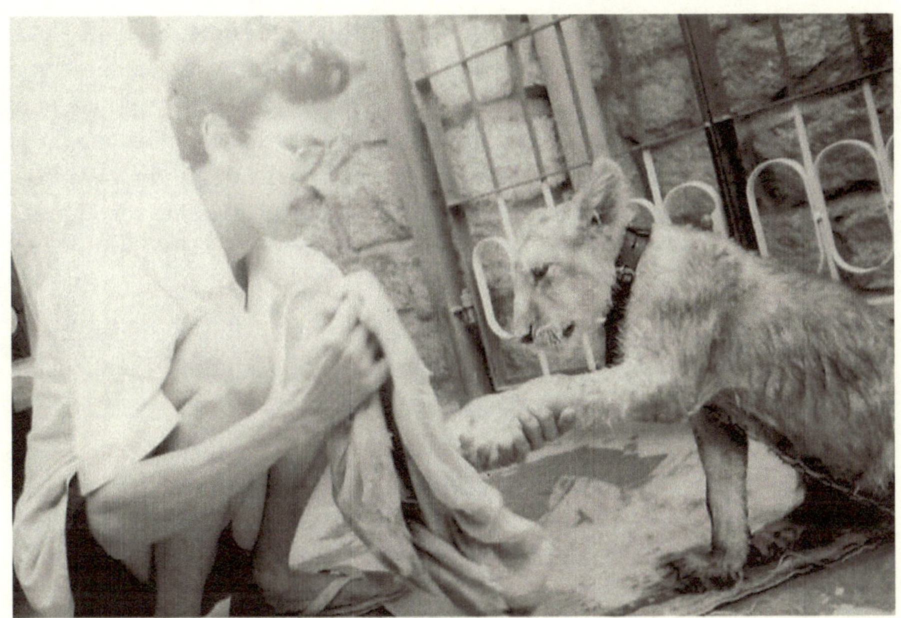

Bath time

Unlike common belief, Sheeba did not give out any body odour. Her coat was always odourless even after a bath. Sheeba did not have a foul breath either unlike other carnivores. It was a pleasurable experience to plant a kiss on Sheeba's nose.

Brushing her coat was also very important. It was enjoyed by the Princess and we would be tired by the end of it. Fortunately, there were no ticks or other ecto-parasites on her. With the good diet Sheeba was on, her coat was really enviable with a lot of sheen and gloss to it. Maybe we could have made an ad for the shampoo and other products which were used on Sheeba.

For recreation and time-pass, Sheeba had a car tyre hung in the niche of the living room where we had the big library cupboard. The carpet was spread at the place and above her was this tyre hanging from the ceiling. When Sheeba was in the mood, she would punch the tyre like boxers do at the sparring bag. The tyre would bounce back equally. This process would go on indefinitely till Sheeba was distracted by something or we would put a stop to it. The best moment for photographers would be the time when Sheeba would put her head through the tyre and rest partially on it. This would remind us of the biggest motion pictures emblem – MGM. The only thing was that Sheeba would not growl like the MGM lion.

Sheeba hardly interacted with other animals at home. She was least interested in the various birds and animals which were rescued and housed in enclosures on the terrace. Our domestic cat, Kitty, was also not of any interest to Sheeba. Evolution-wise she was her smaller cousin in the city. Many a time, Kitty would jump over Sheeba to go her way, least bothered about her big sister in the path. Sheeba, true to being the "Queen of the Jungle," did not give a semblance of a glance to Kitty's antics and would be very aloof.

When free in the compound, our pet street dog, Moti, would come in for her share of petting and pampering from the household. This intrusion also was not noticed by Sheeba in true royal fashion.

One of the days when Sheeba had started eating big slices of meat with bones, she overate and her tummy was bulging as if it was about to burst. Sheeba was really lethargic and found it difficult to move around. When we palpated her belly, we could literally feel the bone pieces as hard masses. We were a little worried as animals generally do not overeat like humans and suffer from a distended abdomen. The only thing to do was to leave Sheeba alone overnight with constant supervision. We could feel that there was much gas in her intestines which had not been let out. Before retiring for the day, we just wanted to ascertain Sheeba's status. Sheeba, on her part, was sleeping on her back and we had clear access to her belly. We thought that by gently massaging her tummy she would find some relief. As we massaged her tummy with our heads over her abdomen, all of us suddenly got the vilest and foulest of smells ever. Sheeba had passed wind. What a smell it was! Even to this day we are able to recollect that smell. Our massage had worked. Sheeba got the much required relief from her suffering. Within a few hours the abdomen had regained its normal contour and we all had a goodnight's sleep.

Inquisitive Sheeba

Sheeba was a typical cat. She would not play "Fetch" like a dog. When a ball or a similar object was thrown, she would run after it and catch it as though it were a prey and would not let go. We had made a small sand bag to simulate prey and Sheeba would play with it for quite some time till she got tired.

Sheeba would be let free in the compound often. When she got bored, she would come to the window of my mother's bedroom and would try to get on to the window sill. Since she was too big, Sheeba would keep her forelegs on the sill and peep into the room. My mother would be doing some embroidery or relaxing in the room. Sheeba would ask to be caressed through the window which my mother would happily oblige.

In her early days while exploring the house, Sheeba had a minor accident. It so happened that in the balcony of the house, Sheeba tried to back herself without noticing where she was going. She had a fall through the railing of the staircase. She did not fall on solid ground, but on plants in the indoor garden. Even then, she could have suffered damage by the mud pots. She had learnt a lesson. A similar incident would not have occurred if Sheeba was older, because the gap in the railings would have been too small for her to fall through.

We have all heard of Pavlov's experiment with respect to a conditioned reflex – ringing of the bell, food for the dog, salivation. He had proved that an animal associates a particular sound, like the ringing of a bell, with food. Similarly, Sheeba had associated the sound of my bike and the opening of the gate with my arrival. One day, my mother noticed Sheeba suddenly stand up with pricked up ears. Within a minute, I entered the house. My mother had noticed that Sheeba was able to recognise the sound of my bike. Sheeba could sense me coming at least from about fifty yards.

In the evening, on coming into the house, after street-watching, Sheeba would sit on a particular sofa in the living room with us and watch television for some time. Whenever she spotted some moving object on the television, she would crane her neck and try to see the images and also listen to the sound, even though it was all gibberish to her ears.

Another favourite spot for Sheeba to relax was the swing. She would get on to the swing and this act itself was enough to keep the momentum of the to and fro movement.

Many visitors would come to see Sheeba and they all had a wonderful time. Some of them came with cameras to shoot the most exciting moment of their lives. Some even came with video cameras. I distinctly remember a boy and a girl in their early twenties coming and standing in front of Sheeba for more than a couple of hours. During the visiting hours, Sheeba would be restrained near the library. It so happened that the girl without her knowledge, moved close to Sheeba. Being within striking distance Sheeba managed to catch hold of the front of the girl's shirt and ripped it. The girl was a little surprised and the remark she made was a good one. Instead of feeling bad at having a good shirt torn, she remarked that she would treasure the shirt forever as a memento.

We had a scooter parked in the compound. Sheeba would stand on the vehicle with her forefeet. Like all cats, she too scratched her nails on objects like tree trunk, door frames, etc. Since the seat of the scooter was soft, she would try to tear the leather cover. As the vehicle was due for service, we went to the workshop. The supervisor there casually asked how come the seat cover was in such a mess. We said that it was ripped open by a lion. He nodded casually. It took him some time for these words to sink in. Once he realised what we had said, he was in utter disbelief. When we repeated that the cause was a lion, his amazement knew no bounds. With his eyes popping out of his sockets, he said he could not believe it. He wanted to visit our house right away and followed us to see Sheeba with his own eyes. This was the type of attraction Sheeba held for the lay man.

One of the days when Sheeba had visitors in the house, we realised that she had somehow managed to get rid of the collar around her neck. It was not very easy to put the collar back and slide the buckle into its slot. Putting back the chain on the collar was easy, but here, the collar itself had given way. Even though Sheeba was well behaved with the family members, we were not sure of her temperament in front of a group of visitors. Collaring Sheeba was done in a very casual and discrete manner. For one, the visitors did not know that Sheeba was free. Secondly and strangely, Sheeba herself did not know that she was free. I walked up to Sheeba who was lying on the carpet and started caressing her. As she lay relaxed without a care in the world, I slowly slipped the collar around her neck and fastened it tightly and put back the chain. Neither Sheeba nor the visitors had realised what had happened.

Only once did Sheeba relieve herself inside the house. It was the cold month of December and the time of the year when sweating is less and frequency of visits to the toilet is more. It was too early in the day for Sheeba to pass urine after her morning ablution. Sheeba, instead of relaxing on the carpet, was standing and looking at us for quite some time. She was trying to convey something to us. None of us realised this.

She was, in fact, asking us to let her out. After waiting for some time, Sheeba relieved herself in the living room itself. The quantity of urine was quite a lot and pungent as well. Poor Sheeba could not keep her sphincter under control. Not her mistake. It was our fault not to have noticed her signal. It required quite an effort to clean the mess on the floor and also the help of a couple of ceiling fans and a fair amount of air freshener to clear the air.

Our neighbours were very friendly and always said that they were a privileged lot to see Sheeba's antics. One of the children, who was about eight, would play with Sheeba, while staying in his compound. This boy would run up and down his compound keeping close to the wall separating our houses. Sheeba would also run up and down in a mock chase. Many a time, he would call Sheeba from across the compound and she would stand on her hind legs and look across the grill at the boy, face-to-face.

As days went by, Sheeba grew well and by the end of the year weighed around eighty kilograms. Her popularity had grown far and wide and people flocked to our residence to have a glimpse of the Princess. Many visitors commented that having a lioness in the house was very unique. Many also said that this was the only instance in India of a family rearing a wild animal like a lioness at home. Some others went to the extent of saying it was the first time in the world.

Free run in the house

There were a lot of articles written on Sheeba in the newspapers, periodicals, magazines, etc. There were television reports too.

In January 1997, my daughter Shruthi, who was nine years old, mentioned that Sheeba would turn one year in February. She suggested having a grand birthday party for the event. We welcomed the idea and soon started preparing for the same. By the end of January, preparations were in full swing because February 6 would be her birthday. The entire house was decorated with buntings, balloons, stickers and also a big board with birthday wishes. We had to rearrange the furniture of the house to accommodate the large number of visitors and the media. We had taken a few extra chairs on hire. We had also arranged high tea for the guests.

The D-Day finally arrived and all of us were very excited. Sheeba was her normal self as she had no knowledge that all these decorations and preparations were for her sake. On February 6, Sheeba was taken outside to the garden. People in the neighbourhood had gotten wind of the event and many were thronging at the gates to see some action. A large number of people from the press, including few reputed publishers descended on the scene quite early in the morning. The television crew of many news and entertainment channels were also present. The big television cameras with lights, wires and microphones were all there jostling for space and to occupy vantage positions for the best pictures and videos.

A prominent five-star hotel in Bangalore presented a huge cake with Sheeba's name and greetings on it. Poor Sheeba had no idea of what was happening. She could not blow the candle and we had to do the needful. A huge round of applause followed the blowing of the candle as cameras flashed. The videographers had their yellow lights on continuously. Each channel reporter could be heard speaking into their respective microphones.

This was one birthday which definitely had surpassed all other celebrations which we had witnessed hitherto. There might have been at least 300 to 500 visitors that day. Everyone went home pleased. All of them had some snacks, spent some time with Sheeba and family members and photographs taken to mark the event. Even today, some eighteen years later, many of these visitors recall that day and everybody says it was something unique and unforgettable. The young children and teenagers who had visited at that time are grown up now with their own children. They tell their children how excited they were when they had seen Sheeba for the first time. Many of them show their children the photographs that they had taken with Sheeba.

The very night of the party, many television channels broadcast the news of Sheeba's first birthday. Everyone had details of how Sheeba was abandoned by her mother and how it came into the Iengar's ARRT. A few days later, some of our friends and relatives rang up from abroad to say that they had watched the programme on Sheeba on BBC channel.

A week after Sheeba's birthday bash, we decided to return her back to BNP. There was a pall of gloom not only in ARRT, but also in the neighbourhood. People in the vicinity were asking us whether Sheeba could manage in the new environment without any familiar people around her.

One thing we have to understand here is that these rescued animals often become misfits. They neither belong totally to their own community nor do they totally adapt among the keepers. Of course, there is scope for a full debate on such a subject. Once the mother does not pay attention to her own offspring, we should know that there is a reason behind this. In nature, such things keep happening very often, but we will not know it. Many a time, among three or four offspring of the animal or bird, one of them is very strong and aggressive and one very meek and timid. It has been seen that the chances of survival of the meek and timid is very low. The mother does not go out of its way to give extra care to such children. The mother knows that such children will not beget healthy offspring and it is best for such animals to die. The idea sounds very harsh for us human beings. It is a fact of Nature. It is only the humans who give so much care and affection to a handicapped animal or bird, or for that matter, another human being.

In the present circumstances one should realise that Sheeba was meant to die. Because of human intervention she was saved. But what happens next? Do we allow Sheeba to mingle with other lions in the park? What if some lioness (may be her own mother) hits out at Sheeba and injures her? Can Sheeba stand a chance? Do we allow Sheeba to be in solitary confinement for the rest of her life without a companion? If she gets familiar with a lion during her stay in the park, do we allow the lion to mingle with her? Do we allow Sheeba to mate with a lion and get pregnant and have a litter with genetic defects again?

These were the problems facing us at the thought of Sheeba going back to the park. On February 12, hardly a week after the birthday function, the Forest Department on our request sent a fairly big metal cage for transporting Sheeba to Bannerghatta. We had made it clear that Sheeba may take her own time to get into the cage and to give us sufficient time to induce her into the cage.

The metal enclosure was left overnight in the compound near the gate of the garden. Seeing the cage, there was a big crowd of curious onlookers. They had all come to see Sheeba off for the last time. Many of them had grown familiar seeing Sheeba roaming the compound. Many of them were emotional and teary-eyed to see Sheeba trans-located. We too were very sad and it was evident on our faces. But, we could not prevent the inevitable. After all, Sheeba was brought to ARRT on the premise that she would be tended to and nursed back to health. Once this was achieved, it was our duty to send Sheeba to her rightful place. But, who would have imagined that Sheeba would develop such a strong emotional bond not only with us but also with the neighbours!

Sheeba was left to familiarize herself with the smell of the new enclosure. She would not get inside the cage. Some sixth sense told Sheeba that entering the cage would be her undoing. Hence, we too did not pressurize her to get into the enclosure by force. We had never used harsh words on Sheeba. There had never been a reason to do so as she was so well behaved. She could always sense what was on our mind without us ordering her. Hence, we did not use any strong arm tactics.

The next morning, February 13, I went as usual to the compound. Sheeba was already there. The gate to the garden was kept open and the enclosure from the Department was also kept open adjacent to the gate. The door of the enclosure had an up-and-down movement to open and shut the cage. I casually went into the cage and sat inside. Sheeba was very wary and would not put her foot inside the cage. I withdrew to the far end of the cage and coaxed Sheeba to come and play with me. After a couple of hours, with great hesitation, Sheeba finally entered the enclosure and someone dropped the cage door. Sheeba and I were both inside. I did not try to come out immediately. In fact, I spent quite some time playing with her in a reassuring way that nothing was amiss. The carpet on which Sheeba used to sleep was put inside the cage so that some familiar smelling object would be inside with her to comfort her.

FIRST DAY AT THE PARK: Once the Forest Department personnel arrived with a big vehicle to transport Sheeba, we were ready to follow them to the park. The crowd that had collected near the gates of ARRT and along the streets reminded me of my childhood days when Queen Elizabeth visited Bangalore's M.G. Road. The whole of M.G. Road was thronging with people to greet the Queen. And here was our own Queen of the Jungle as the centre of attraction. Apart from us, the crowd was also concerned about the welfare of Sheeba being in an isolated environment.

We had to reassure them that it was for the good of Sheeba in the long run. There would be a transitional phase of uncertainty and anxiety for both Sheeba and us which had to be borne stoically.

The big vehicle with Sheeba in the enclosure started off to Bannerghatta. ARRT members followed them. There were no untoward incidents along the twenty kilometre route. The journey took about an hour. The personnel at the park were expecting Sheeba's arrival and had already made the necessary arrangements.

The presence of a new animal at a distance was immediately noticed by the inmates and roars and growls could be heard from a distance. These sounds were totally alien to Sheeba and made her very nervous. The enclosure of Sheeba was brought as close to the cells of the lions as possible. Sheeba had to be taken by walk during the last stretch. All the people around were anxious and scared about the outcome. Somehow, I had the confidence that Sheeba would not misbehave or throw a tantrum. The first and foremost thing that was done was to pacify Sheeba. She had to understand that she was amidst her own clan. Since Sheeba was attached to me the most, I took the initiative. I started calling out to Sheeba and caressed her through the enclosure. This gave her a lot of confidence. I reassured the Forest Personnel that nothing untoward would happen and asked them to open the enclosure door. There was no cover at this place so Sheeba had to be walked on a leash to her designated cell. As she emerged from the enclosure, I snapped the chain to her collar and hugged her. I also put my thumb into her mouth. This was very pacifying for Sheeba. We could sense through her body language that her fear of the unknown had come down. We gave her sufficient time to take stock of the situation. All of us caressed Sheeba to reassure her once again. We made her walk along the narrow corridor to her allocated cell. The smell of the other lions was overbearing for us. For Sheeba, who had a sensitive nose, this scent must have been a hundredfold more. The growls and roars of other inmates were deafening. I had my thumb inside Sheeba's mouth for her to suckle on, as and when she showed signs of nervousness.

Sheeba's cell was fairly big with a small recess on one side with a cement tank with water. Initially, Sheeba and I went inside. The collapsible gate was closed. The floor was of solid granite stones. The backyard of the cell was also quite big. It was covered with wet mud for the felines to relieve themselves. The rest of ARRT and a couple of Forest Personnel came inside later. Sheeba's chain was removed with only the collar on her. I led Sheeba to the recess where there was water. She immediately started quenching her thirst. The journey and the accompanying fear and anxiety had made Sheeba very thirsty. She drank quite a lot. When food was offered she hardly noticed it and wanted to be comforted. After this, Sheeba appeared a little settled.

Our family members were comfortable inside the cell with Sheeba. The caretakers were quite nervous to be in the company of Sheeba. Even though they were well-versed in looking after the other inmates of the lion enclosure, they were very uneasy at the sight of a lioness roaming free amidst us. We, of course, were comfortable with Sheeba freely moving in the cell. We had to keep reassuring the Department personnel about the behaviour of Sheeba. We had to instruct the keepers about Sheeba's daily routine - what she ate and how much and at what time. We stayed for about two or three hours with her, giving her quality time. Sheeba did not show any interest in the food offered, which we had brought from the house. The Department people also offered her the food which was given to other lions.

We had a feeling that Sheeba knew that we were going to leave her in isolation and go away. She would try to catch hold of my trousers in her big paws and refuse to let go. We had to manipulate our moves such that one by one, all the members in the cell went out and I was left alone with Sheeba. We had spent more than three to four hours with her and we decided it was better to leave her alone to rest, with due instructions to the Department staff regarding Sheeba's requirements.

I slowly disentangled Sheeba's forefoot from my trousers and began inching away towards the exit of the collapsible gate. I kept a constant barrage of sweet little nothings to keep Sheeba in good spirits. Then, I had to make a small dash to the exit and close the doors behind me. We all felt bad in isolating Sheeba this way. But, it was for her good in the long run. Once we were all outside we bid goodbye with a heavy heart. On our drive back home, the conversation was all about how Sheeba would cope with the new environment. We had made sure that the big round carpet was spread out in her cell so that she would have a little smell of her earlier surroundings.

The evening at home was very dull and boring. We had all been so used to Sheeba in our daily routine that we all missed her presence very much. None of us had an appetite for dinner. We did not have a peaceful sleep as well. The next day we all wished Sheeba a happy morning in absentia. We were eager to visit her in her new home. We had early lunch to enable us to visit her as early as possible. We packed "lunch" for Sheeba also as we knew that she would not touch the food provided by the park.

As we drove towards the enclosures of the lions, our hearts were pumping with excitement in anticipation of spending time with our Princess. After parking our car we had to walk a small distance towards the enclosure. We started calling Sheeba's name aloud to make her know that we were nearby. We all heard a series of loud anguished growls. This was repeated several times till we reached the enclosure of Sheeba. We all hurried up. The keeper lost no time in opening the cell door. Sheeba was frantic to meet us and made no bones in showing her excitement and affection. The moment we entered the cell, Sheeba stood up on her hind limbs and put both front feet on my shoulders. Sheeba's huge face was in front of mine and she was trying to brush her head against my face. One could see the love and affection in her lovely eyes. She even made a few attempts to lick my face. Sheeba was so overcome with emotion that she kept whining like a dog. After all of us had a go at Sheeba, she finally settled down.

Once the excitement had died down, it was time for us to feed Sheeba. We opened her lunch box. The department staff had also kept a bowl with egg and meat in the enclosure. Sheeba had not shown any interest in consuming it. Sheeba was not interested in eating her own 'home food' also. All that she wanted to do was to spend some quality time with us. We had to cajole her into eating small pieces from the box. We are all used to seeing lions in the wild rushing towards a kill and eating with frenzy and infighting. Even zoo animals show great excitement at the arrival of the keeper with the food and waste no time in gobbling up all the food. Growling noises are made and they are very irritable during this period. Sheeba was just the opposite. No growls or snarls for her. It was just tender loving care and coaxing that worked for her. The enclosure of Sheeba had a collapsible door on the back side which led to a large area covered with mud. The cell had granite slabs all over. The mud surface would enable Sheeba to smell the earth and relieve herself.

After spending a couple of hours, it was time for us to return home. Sheeba would again sense that we were about to exit and tried to block the exit. She would stand near the exit and also try to catch hold of my trousers. It was difficult to deceive her in some manner and get out of the enclosure. To make amends, we would all stand outside the cell and pet Sheeba through the grill for sometime before bidding a final farewell for the day.

The news hounds were not to be left behind in covering Sheeba's story. Many news channels and newspaper reporters wanted to continue the story after her birthday which was fresh in their minds. They were all eager to fire questions. Sure enough they came in thick and fast. How was Sheeba's health? Was she eating well? Was she being looked after properly? Was she allowed to go with other lions? How was she behaving with the new keepers? Was she in depression? The best thing to do was to invite these reporters to Bannerghatta and allow them to see for themselves the state of affairs and also ask them to speak with the officials.

After release at Bannerghatta National Park

Two or three days later, there was plenty of news in the newspapers, the local TV and National News channels that Sheeba was on hunger strike and her health was deteriorating. The reporters even went to the extent of interviewing the Forest Department Minister. They demanded to know from the minister as to what steps were being taken to safeguard Sheeba's health. Of course, it was a matter of time before things could settle down. The first week after Sheeba's translocation we made it a point to visit her every day in the afternoon and spend a couple of hours. The plan was to slowly wean Sheeba away from our influence and make her go with her own pride. This was not as easy as said. After about ten days, when we skipped a day, there were phone calls from the Forest Department saying that Sheeba had not eaten the food given by the department.

The next plan was to mix a little food of the Forest Department with the food we were taking for Sheeba. Gradually, over a period of a few days, the proportion of the department food would be increased and ultimately, in a matter of couple of months, we hoped that we would put a stop to our visits. Then on, Sheeba would be eating only the food provided by the department. Who has not heard of Elsa the lioness that featured in the 1960s movie 'Born Free?' There are books on Elsa the lioness – 'Born Free, Living Free and Forever Free.' The actress who tends to Elsa in the movie – Virginia McKenna – started an organisation called Born Free Foundation to fund many animal shelters across the world.

Well, Virginia was in contact with our ARRT during Sheeba's stay in our premises. In fact, she was making a visit to Bangalore to oversee the maintenance of the three tigers which were brought from London to BNP. Virginia came to see whether sufficient space and facilities were given to them. She was supposed to stay for a couple of days in Bangalore. When we offered our own premises for her boarding and lodging, she immediately accepted the invitation.

On her visit to Bangalore, she was thrilled and overjoyed to see the work ARRT had done in the last fifteen years. She went through all the photographs and videos of the animals which had been rehabilitated in the centre. Sheeba had just been returned to the park and Virginia was very happy seeing the photographs showing the development of Sheeba from a sick animal to a robust queen of the jungle.

We had told Virginia that we would take her to the park to see the London tigers and meet the Forest Department officials regarding the same. We also took her to see Sheeba. She was so excited after seeing Sheeba that she became nostalgic and started recollecting her younger days during the shooting of the film 'Born Free.' She related many of her experiences during the shoot and also how mischievous Elsa had been. Virginia had to get back to London and she had a lot of memories of her stay with ARRT and Sheeba at the park to take back home. Virginia's visit invigorated us to step up our activities further.

Many of our friends and relations who were close to Sheeba wanted to go with us to see her. Every time we went to visit Sheeba, there would be another three or four people in another vehicle, accompanying us. They would watch me play with Sheeba inside the enclosure. Sheeba was always her old self. She would catch hold of my trousers and not let go. She would also gently sink her teeth into my leg without hurting me. Many people were of the opinion that I had some sort of a protective covering over my legs under my trousers which prevented Sheeba's fangs from sinking into my flesh.

Once, one of our colleagues wanted to go with us to see Sheeba. They had brought a camera and wanted to take pictures of Sheeba. We all set out in the morning. Sheeba as usual was very happy to see us. We convinced our friends to come inside the enclosure so that the pictures could be taken better without the grillwork being seen in the photographs. They were bold enough to come inside. Sheeba was least bothered about the presence of others and went on playing with me. My friend started taking photographs. Sheeba and I gave good poses for the camera. After a couple of hours we thought of winding up the photo shoot. We bid goodbye to Sheeba. My friend's camera was not the digital kind. One had to load it with color films of thirty-six exposures. The older generation would know this. It was not the digital era yet. After a week or so I was keen to see the photographs. When I asked for the same, my friend was crestfallen. It was a shock for me to know that the camera was NOT LOADED. There was no film in it. The camera which boasted of so many features did not recognise that there was no film. One could go on clicking photos and the counter would keep changing numbers also. This gave an impression that the film was moving to the next frame. Imagine when they went to the photo shop to give the film for development and printing, only to find that there was no film. I felt very bad because we would have had some really good shots of Sheeba for posterity.

The process of visiting Sheeba continued for another three to four months. The frequency of our visits gradually reduced and ultimately, at the end of a year we stopped visiting Sheeba. The only news we would get occasionally was from the zoo keepers who would call up to say that everything was alright. Slowly, the memories of Sheeba started fading. Our only consolation was the videos and photographs of her, which would keep us pre-occupied. After a period of some ten to twelve years we got to know of the sad demise of Sheeba. We were not sure of the exact date and time also. Even to this day we keep recollecting the good old days by going through the album and watching the videos of Sheeba. We remember her all the more on her birthday every year.

First encounter with a young
Sheeba at Bannerghatta National Park

A malnourished Sheeba

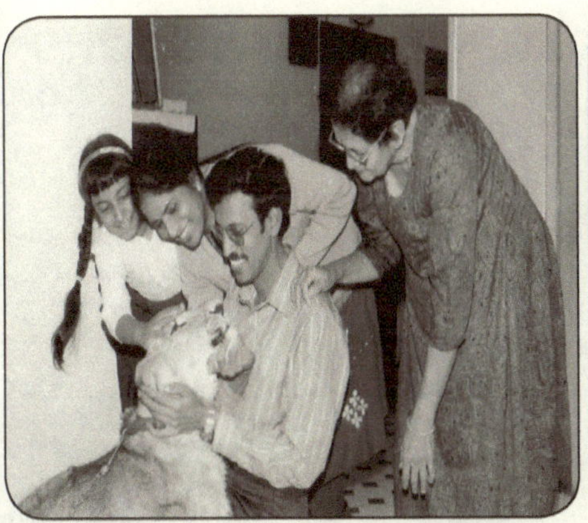

The Iengar Family with Sheeba

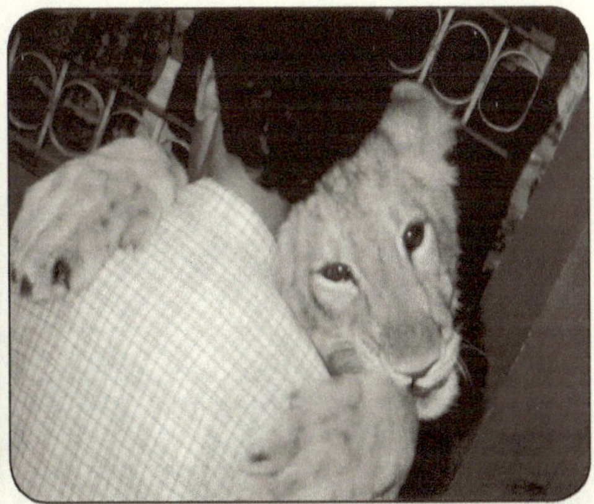

Hug of the century

Shashidhar planting a
kiss on Sheeba's nose

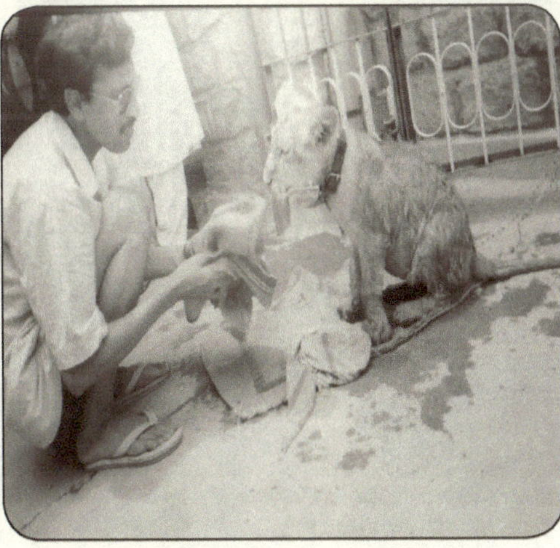

Sheeba enjoying her bath

Mimicking MGM productions

Playing with sheeba

On her favourite carpet

Relaxing

Prowling in the garden

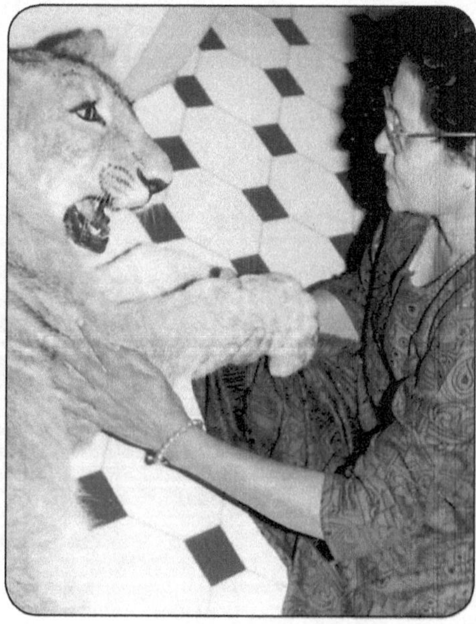

Sheeba playing with Janaki Iengar

Janaki Iengar and Sheeba

Sheeba at the gate

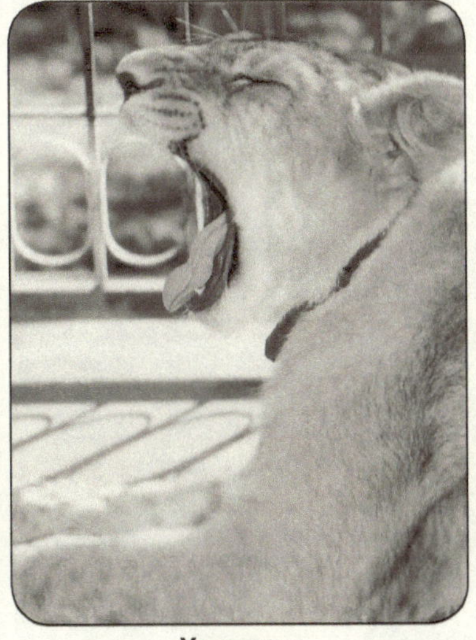

Yaaaawn

Happy Birthday

At Bannerghatta after release

African lovebird young- feeding

African lovebird adult

Cobra young

Cobra-Spectacled variety

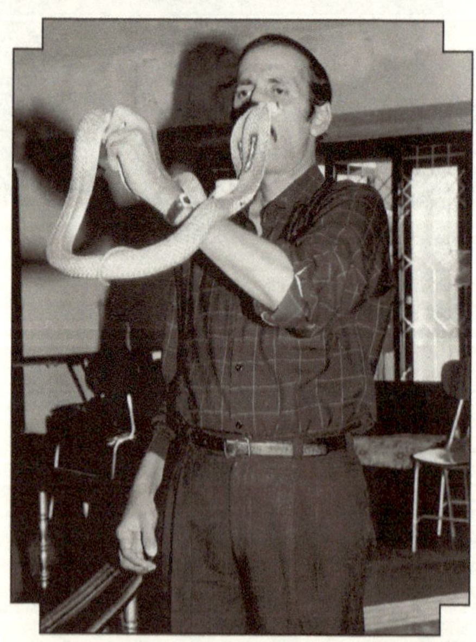

Cobra adult being handled by Srinath

Barn owl chicks

Barn owl adults

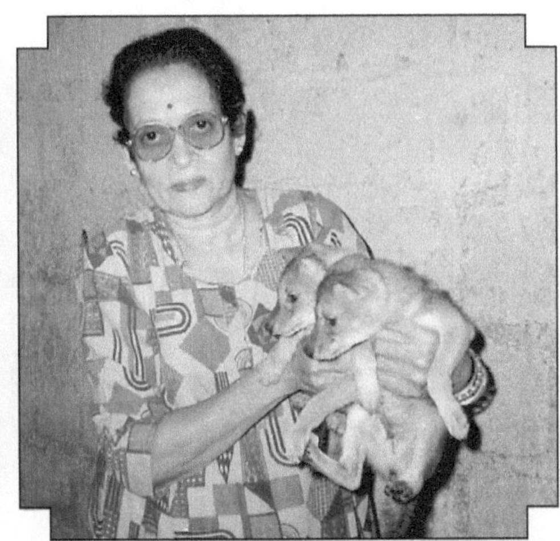

Jackal cubs

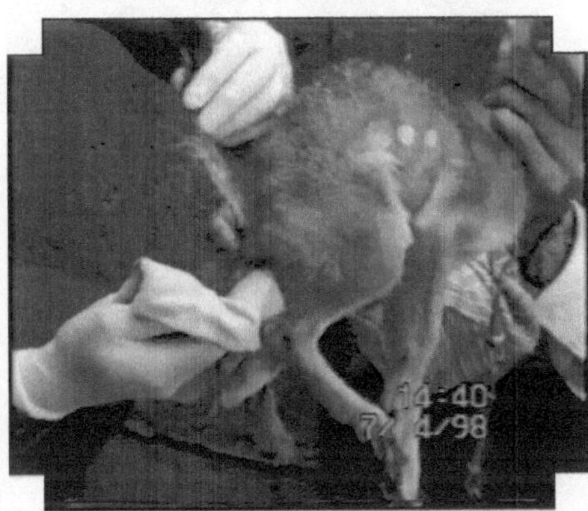

Jackal with prolapse

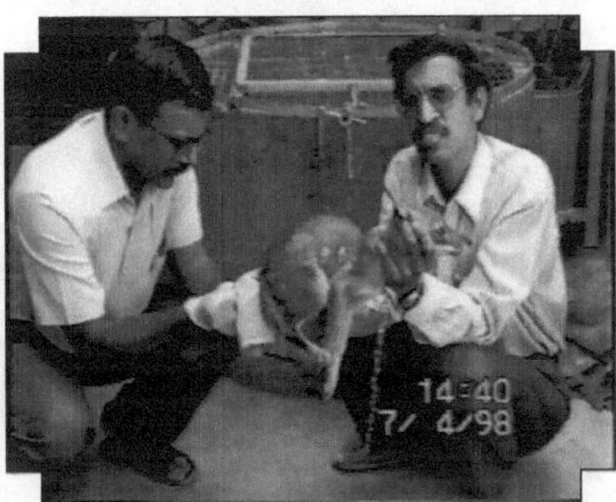

Jackal surgery

Jackal Adult

Kestrel just freed

Kestrel which returned

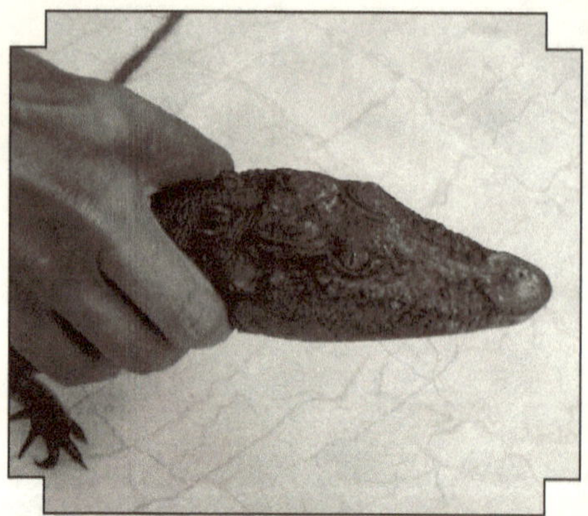

Crocodile young

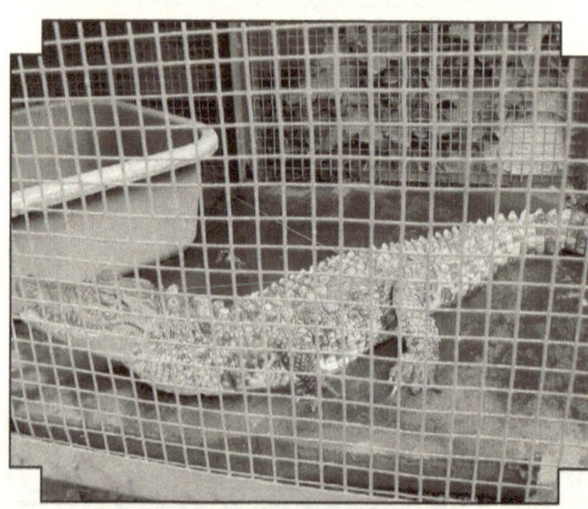

Crocodile - 6 months old

Chameleon

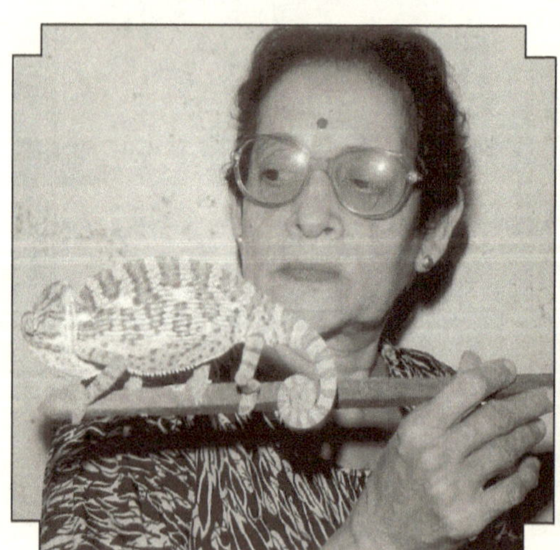

Chameleon changing colors

Alexandrine Parakeet

Barbet's foot with hardened excreta

Parakeet -blind from young age

Rose - ringed Parakeet

Cockatiel

Brahminy kite

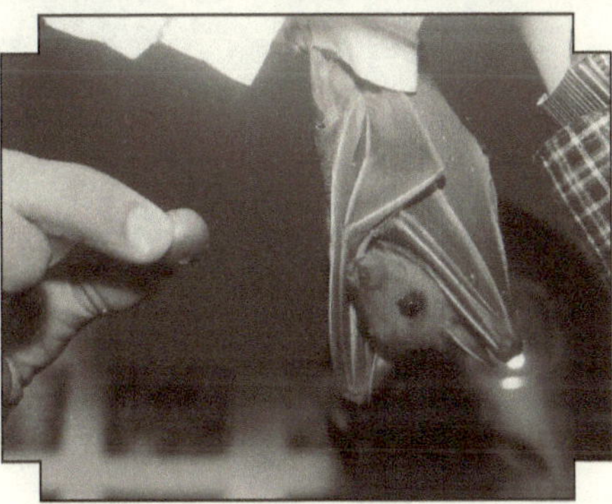

Fruit bat

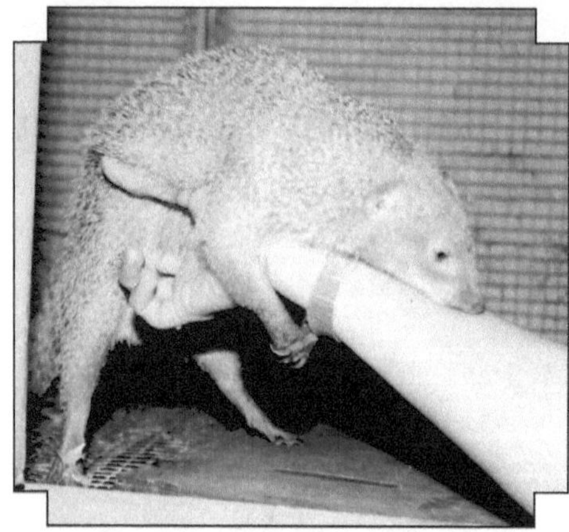

Mongoose

Great Indian Horned Owl

Mottled wood owl

Monkey with pup

Mynah

Night Heron

Pangolin

Piggy enjoying curd rice

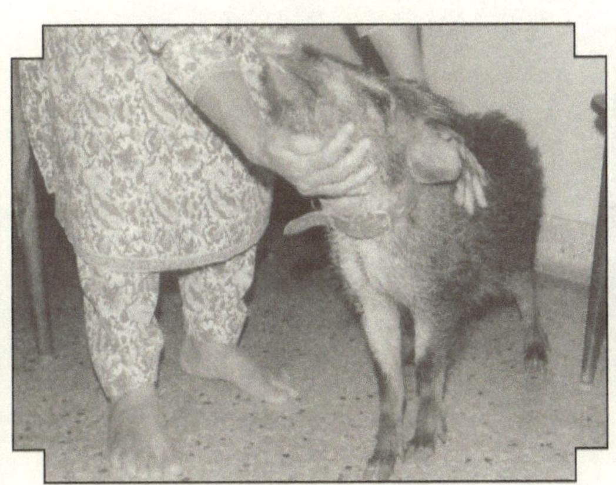

Piggy - the Wild Boar

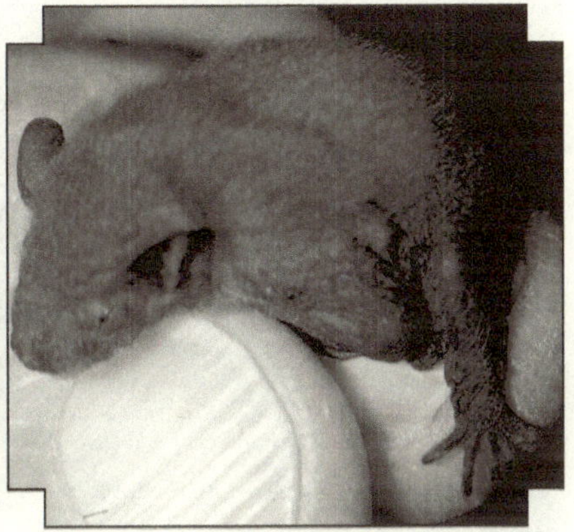

Pipistrelle

Pitta

Python

Rat snake with eggs

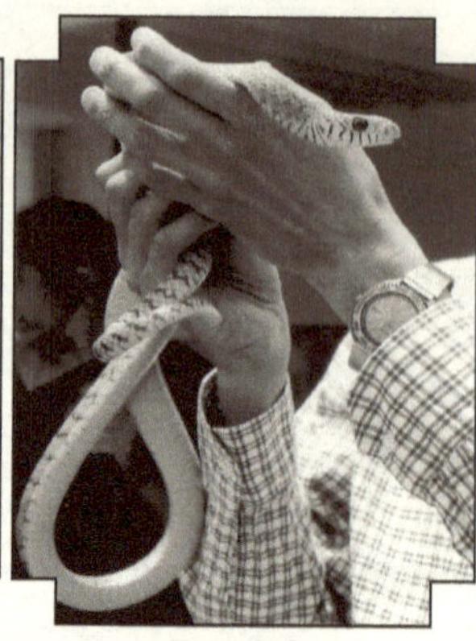

Rat snake

Red-eared turtle

Royal snake

Russell's viper

Sand boa

Slender Loris

Spotted deer with Mrs. Iengar

Srinath handling a King Cobra

Toddy cat

Turtles

SNAKES

The first encounter with a wild snake was quite interesting. A small brown colored snake with black stripes was seen moving along the compound wall. The first reaction of all of us was a little fear and also curiosity. My brother Srinath and my father, M K S Iengar was there at the gate and observed it first. Srinath wanted to capture the snake and study it. He shouted to me to bring a broom to trap the snake and put it in a container. Being inside the house I could not make out from where my brother was calling. Mistaking it to be upstairs, I ran up the steps only to find the terrace deserted. I peered down the parapet to see them at the gate. I threw the broom down to them and ran down myself. With great agility the snake was trying to dodge the broom and slip away into a crevice nearby. We were afraid that it was poisonous. We had very little knowledge about snakes in general and did not know that there were only four important poisonous snakes in India. Somehow we guided the snake into a big glass jar and quickly put the lid on it. We made a few holes for ventilation on the plastic lid.

The first thing that we observed was that the snake was putting out its tongue frequently and moving around the base of the jar restlessly. We observed that the eyes were quite big and it had a staring gaze. We realised that this was because it had no eyelids. Maybe this was the reason people believed that snakes could hypnotise people. The tongue was also very peculiar. It was split at the tip and appeared like a double tongue. We could not make out why the tongue kept forking out so often. It was only after reading up some literature that we came to know about the chemical senses transmitted from the atmosphere to the Jacobson's organ at the roof of the mouth. This acted like a dog's nose to smell the surroundings and tell the snake about the presence of prey, predator, water or any other danger.

We had a few primitive books on snakes which gave information about basic things, such as that there are only four poisonous snakes in India – Cobra, Russell's Viper, Saw-scaled Viper and the Krait, apart from the King Cobra. We learnt through a black and white photograph that this snake was relatively common and non-poisonous. Its name was Striped Keel Back. Once we realised that the specimen was non-poisonous, we decided to put it out on the table and see what it would do. We opened the lid of the jar and tilted it so that the snake could slip out. We did not make any sudden movements to disturb the snake. We observed how it could slide its belly scales to move forward. Since the snake did not show any tendency to lunge and bite we put our hand at the edge of the table for the snake to slide on to our hands. The snake behaved as though our hand was an inanimate object and started moving up the forearm. The snake moved on to the other hand when held out. This way we were able to juggle the snake between two hands. We had heard people say that snakes were slimy. This was not the case. The snake was very slippery because of its smooth and streamlined body but not slimy. There was no smell either. Observing its sedate nature we could correlate why this snake was called the gentleman snake.

After a few hours we put a small container with water and manoeuvred the snake towards it. Our legless friend slowly slithered towards the water and put its mouth on the surface and started drinking. We could make out the sides of the jaw contracting and relaxing and thereby sucking the water into its mouth. This process went on for a couple of minutes. By night after having studied the snake for some time we decided to give freedom to our friend. We released the snake at the same spot where we had found it. The snake crawled into the bushes in the garden and made itself invisible in no time.

This one incident was the turning point in our lives because this little creepy crawly had generated a lot of interest in all of us to start studying in detail about snakes and other reptiles. At that time there was no free access to information like our modern day internet and Google. We had to go to the library nearby or buy the books from some good bookshop. Each one of the family members would read up about different aspects of the snake and discuss the same in the evening free time. This way there was good exchange of knowledge and faster learning about the subject.

This was the time in the mid-seventies when there were many snake charmers moving around in the city. They would be carrying with them cobras which had been defanged and rendered harmless. They would also put up on display non-poisonous snakes like the Rat Snake, boas, pythons and sometimes the green colored Vine Snake. These snake charmers were very good in putting up road side show for the public and collect money for their living. Even though we had seen these acts being performed, we had not shown much interest. Now after this snake encounter we took a special interest in the goings on. We asked one of the snake charmers to come home with his pets and put up a show for us exclusively. Khasim, the charmer, agreed.

I would not be understating it if I said that through Khasim, we learnt so many facts about snakes which would have been difficult to absorb through a regular book on snakes. These snake charmers had learnt these facts from their forefathers. He told us how a cobra is caught in the wild. He mentioned that in India, people come across cobras and vipers mainly and the vipers were very dangerous compared to the cobra. He told us how, immediately after catching the cobra, the venom gland and the fangs would be removed with a small razor blade without much harm to the snake. Of course, it was another matter that the snake could not catch its normal prey and would starve to death but for the artificial milk and egg mixture which would be forced down the throat of the defanged cobra. This nutrition would make the snake survive for some two to three months. Enough time for the snake charmer to make some money. The cobra would slowly get weak and die and the snake charmer would catch another cobra and go through the same routine. When confronted the snake charmer would show another cobra and lie to us that it is the same cobra which we had seen earlier. There was no way one could identify the individual snake.

Khasim also told us what we had known earlier. He said that the cobra would not dance to the music of the flute but rather follow the movement of the flute which made it appear that the snake was dancing to the music. We had learnt that snakes are deaf to air-borne sounds and had no external ear or an opening like a lizard. Snakes, of course, can feel the vibrations picked up from the ground as in the case of movement of prey or predator. This was one reason people moving around in the snake infested area are told to wear some footwear which makes some noise and create

Young Cobra

vibration in the ground. This will alert the snake in the vicinity to move out of the path of the vibration. Villagers who do not wear footwear are the ones who are likely to be bitten by snakes because the victim comes unannounced in the path of the snake and the poor snake inflicts a bite out of pure self-defence.

Khasim was a very learned person in the sense that he had practical knowledge of snakes and other wild animals. He had two boas with him. The boa usually brings to mind huge snakes which are referred to as boa constrictor, anaconda and such else. Of course, they belong to the same boa family. Whereas the Anacondas are huge snakes, Khasim's pet boas were quite small. They are called the red boa or the two-headed snake. The funny thing about these red boas is that they have a round tail, unlike most snakes which have a tapered tail. In fact, the folklore is that these snakes have two heads. Half the year the head is on one end and it switches sides during the second half. There is a bit of a scientific fact which we should understand to know the reason for the myth. These red boas are bright red and they are burrowing snakes. Their habit is to burrow in the mud with their head inside and their tail sticking out a little on the surface. The snake adds a little bit of a wagging movement to the exposed tail which makes any animal passing by including humans to think that the tail end is the head. Animals may bite the tail or the human may give a blow to it thinking that the vital part of the snake is injured. In fact, this is a ploy by the snake to deceive its enemies. Many people believe that the snake eats mud. But, In fact, this snake along with other species found on the farmland devours rats and helps the farmer in pest control and greater produce of harvest.

Khasim told us about the common snakes that are encountered. He had a Rat Snake which was about seven or eight feet in length and very well behaved. He said that on initially catching a Rat Snake they bite repeatedly and cause a lot of damage, even though there is no poison. Over a period of time and repeated handling the rat snake slowly gets acclimatised to the touch of the human and starts behaving. The eyes of the Rat Snake are huge compared to other snakes. This is because the Rat Snake is arboreal-tree dwelling. They also venture on the ground to catch rats as the name suggests. They are very good friends of the farmer. Many farmers feel that these rat snakes are dangerous to them and kill them without realising the benefit of their presence in the fields and in the granary. In many parts of the world the Rat Snakes are kept in the granaries on purpose to reduce the effect of the rat menace. Rats not only eat the grains but also make the grains unfit for consumption by soiling it with their excreta. People with good knowledge of snakes can easily distinguish between a Rat Snake and a cobra. Even though the coloring of the two is similar, the cobra has a distinct hood. On close scrutiny, the pattern of markings is also different. But for a lay man, these things are indistinguishable. Also, many are of the opinion that the Rat Snake and cobra are one and the same. In fact, the story goes that the cobra is the male and the Rat Snake is the female of the same species. Such ignorance!

It is to be understood that each species of snakes can mate with their own species. Their reproductive organs are made to match with their own kind and it is impossible for one species to mate with another. Khasim was good enough to give his collection of snakes to us so that we could make a study of them. Snake charmers had containers made out of bamboo. They would keep the different snakes in these boxes. But, we wanted to keep the snakes in open glass containers so that we could study their habits and behaviour. The first thing that came to our minds was a fish tank with a lid which was properly fitting so that the snakes could not escape from the glass tank. We were able to procure half a dozen of the fish tanks – aquariums. We checked whether there were any gaps and then let each of the snakes into individual glass tanks. Depending upon the species we put variable amount of sand and mud in the enclosures. Burrowing snakes like the Sand Boas had a thick layer of sand whereas the Rat Snakes and Vine snakes had less. The Rat Snake tank was big to accommodate the seven-footer. Vine snakes had small tree branches put in to feel at home. The Green Vine Snakes immediately climbed on to the branches and tried to camouflage themselves among the green foliage. Water snakes were also there which were about a foot in length. They were provided with a big bowl of water in which they preferred to stay. Of course, water in small bowls was provided for all the snakes.

Green Keelback

We all were very interested in the activities of the new comers and were thrilled to have a collection of snakes. We were amateurs. We made observations and prepared notes on the happenings. We observed how the Rat Snake could inflate its body a great deal when agitated. How was this achieved? Very simple. Just take in a deep breath and hold. Since the lung occupies two thirds of the length of the body the snake nearly doubles in size. This display would put fear among its prey and even among its predator – man. The same deep breath technique changes the markings on the Green Vine Snake. The totally green snake would have black checks decorating its body and with its mouth open showing its pink inside would put terror in the hearts of the enemies. Add to this the vicious lunge from the branch of a tree and any animal including a human would take to his heels in no time.

Two or three days later, we were slowly getting accustomed to the new guests in the house. We had made notes of what all was transpiring in those glass tanks. One important thing which we had all forgotten was that these guests were living beings like us and required energy to go about their daily routine. Where does the energy come from? Of course, through the food! And where was the food coming for the guests. Three days had passed and there was no food for the guests? Is this the way one looks after the guests? None of us had found out from Khasim as to what these snakes ate and when. When the realisation dawned on us, the first thing we wanted was Khasim. Imagine our surprise when the bell rang and Khasim was at the door! He too had realised the problem and had come with the solution. We told Khasim to take the snakes which needed to be fed and bring them back later. Khasim told us that the water snakes would eat frogs. The Rat Snakes also eat frogs and rats. The Vine Snake preferred the garden lizards.

We thought that this was the best time to rearrange the contents of the tank. The water bowl had become a little green with the growth of algae. The water itself had dust floating on it. It was high time we changed the water and also cleaned the bowl. The first time we put our hand inside the enclosure with the snake inside was nerve-wracking. Khasim kept on telling that the snake would not do anything but we had our own doubts. At last, the bowl was out and it was cleaned and fresh water kept back. The same was repeated for all the snake enclosures and at the end of it we were quite tired mentally.

Khasim returned with the well fed snakes after a couple of days and we again put them back into their respective containers. The feeding of the cobra was a problem. The cobra which Khasim had given us was defanged and had no poison fangs or venom glands. As soon as a cobra was caught in the wild by pinning down the head of the snake, at the same instant the snake charmer would pull out the fangs and also make a small cut inside the mouth to take off the venom glands on both sides. This would render the poisonous cobra completely harmless. If only the fangs of the snake are removed they would grow back in a matter of days and the snake would be poisonous within no time.

The cobra or any other poisonous snake depends upon the venom to kill its prey. Unlike the non-poisonous snake like the Rat Snake or Water Snake, a cobra will not eat a prey like a frog or rat if it is wriggling. The method adopted by the poisonous snake is to bite the victim and allow it to escape. With the help of its split tongue, the snake will track down the prey to wherever it has gone. By this time the venom would have acted and the prey would be dead or motionless. The snake then makes sure that the prey is really not going to move by nudging it with its head. The prey is then swallowed head first without any chewing and biting.

When the snake is defanged and rendered harmless, the prey continues to run away and the snake can never catch it. Poisonous snakes for some reason cannot hold on to a struggling prey. Only the Water Snake and the Rat Snake can do so.

Over a period of time, all the family members got over the unfounded fear of snakes. All that was required was knowledge regarding the snakes to dispel all the myths which had been passed on to us from our forefathers. Khasim taught us how to catch a cobra in the wild and how to avoid getting bitten in the process. One thing which is very clear is that catching a cobra was easier than catching a non-poisonous snake like Water Snake or a Rat Snake. Once you have studied the behaviour of the different species of snakes, it becomes very evident that the cobra is the most predictable snake. The Rat Snake, Water Snake and the like twist, turn and lunge in the most unpredictable manner. The handler can easily get bitten by these snakes. The cobra when on the ground during encounter will stop moving and lift its hood and hiss loudly to scare the predator. Only when the predator is in striking distance will the cobra lunge forward and inflict a bite. This repeated movement of raising the hood, and then lunging for the bite is predictable. On encountering a cobra in the wild, one has to be courageous in the first place to attempt catching it. A stick of about two feet length will come in handy to pin down the head of the cobra. The next step is to hold the tail with a good grip and not let it slither away. One need not actually hold the head of the cobra with the fingers. Once the cobra is lifted off the ground by holding the tail, it will try to move up and come close to the handler. This can be easily tackled with the help of the stick. Another bold person with a gunny bag or a pillow cover is needed to guide the snake into the bag. Once the snake is put inside the bag, the tail should not be pushed into the bag immediately. Many a time, the snake will have good support at the bottom of the bag and unless the bag is very big, it will try to bite the hand when the tail is being shoved in. Snakes generally prefer darkness and like to get away from bright light and this makes the snake get into a bag which is quite dark and cosy.

The catching of non-poisonous snakes is relatively difficult because of their extreme agility and unpredictability of movement. Method of catching depends on the situation where the snake is encountered. Also, once these snakes get a grip on the victim they bite repeatedly like as if they are chewing on some food. A very interesting way to catch these snakes is to throw a big towel over the head of the snake and blind it. The snake tries to hide inside the towel or tries to get out of it. This gives sufficient time for the handler to move in and grip the head of the snake along with the towel and later release it where required. This way one can avoid getting bitten. These snakes do leave you with very nasty bites. Even though there is no venom, you can expect quite a lot of bleeding. A shot of tetanus toxoid is a must for all these types of non-poisonous snake bites.

Catching a viper is really dangerous and requires expertise and knowledge. There are two types of vipers found in India: the Russell's Viper and the Saw-scaled Viper. The Russell's Viper is a big snake and many people fear this because as the legend goes even the breath of this snake is poisonous and causes decay. Of course, the poison of the viper and not the breath causes rotting of the flesh. The Saw-scaled Viper as the name indicates has the markings of a saw along the side of its body. The saw-scaled is quite small measuring hardly a foot when fully grown but with the same deadly venom as the other vipers. The vipers are highly evolved when compared to the cobras in that the fang mimics

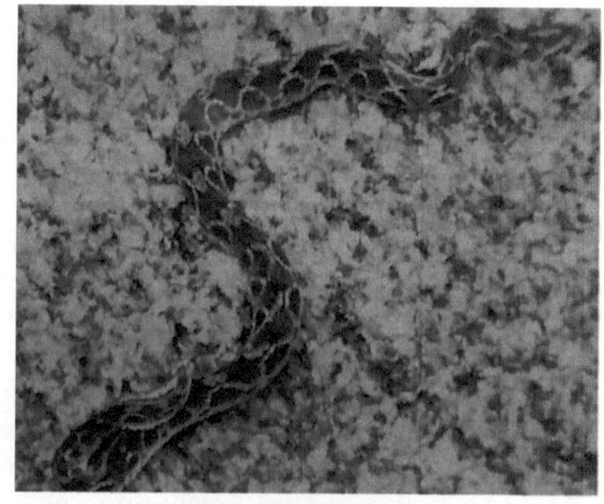

Saw-scaled viper

the hypodermic needle used by the doctors. There is no wastage of venom and the bites of vipers are very effective. Also, the venom of vipers acts on the blood by preventing clotting unlike the cobra venom which is neurotoxic affecting the nervous system and causing death by respiratory failure.

We, my brother Srinath and I, have had many encounters with snakes. They include cobras, Rat Snakes, Russell's Viper, Saw-scaled Viper, water snakes etc. Among us we must have caught at least a couple of hundred snakes. Even though each instance of snake catching was an experience in itself, I vividly remember about a dozen of them which were unique.

Let me narrate some of the episodes in detail so that you could also be involved in these unique circumstances. After becoming adept in catching poisonous snakes, we started taking calls from people in distress where snakes had entered their premises and caused panic among the inhabitants. We would go together most of the times and help the inmates by professionally catching the reptile and giving peace of mind to the inmates.

1. One of the instances that come to my mind is the call we received from a resident of Jayanagar, 4th Block, Bangalore. This house was located close to the bus stop and having a lot of human and vehicular traffic even during the 1980s, when this happened. The inmate of the house told us over phone that a snake was spotted by his father who was in his 80s. He also mentioned that his father was having a little dementia and his words could not be taken seriously. Anyway, he wanted us to check out about the presence of the snake. We agreed and visited the house. We asked the elderly man to explain what exactly happened. He told us that just before entering the pooja room he spotted a cobra slithering behind a photo frame of a Goddess in the veranda. He wanted to tell the others but forgot and started doing pooja. After a couple of hours, he suddenly remembered the incident and shared it with others. But, the others were sceptical about it. We immediately asked for a stool to see what was behind the frame. We put a stick behind the frame and shook it vigorously. Nothing happened. Then, we saw that there was a big plastic bag behind the frame and lots of paper was stuffed into it. We brought down the plastic bag slowly and cautioned the people to move away just in case. To our surprise, there was this huge four and a half foot cobra happily relaxing inside the plastic bag. We made room for ourselves to let the snake out and catch it in the traditional manner and put it into a cloth bag which we had brought for the purpose. The inmates of the house were stunned to find such a big poisonous snake in their house, that too in such a crowded locality. The elderly man was the only one who was proud. He had proved it beyond doubt to the other members that his memory was in place and no longer a matter of ridicule, except that the memory came a little late. But, better late than never as the idiom goes.

2. This call was from a close friend of ours. He had a palatial house in Jayanagar and again in a busy locality. He called to say that he had spotted a snake in his larder. This was adjacent to the kitchen and when we entered it we saw a lot of excreta of the rats. The mesh of the window was damaged and the rats had started pillaging the various edible things in the larder. The cobra had smelt the rats and had come to feast on as many of them as possible. The cook had gone to fetch something from the larder when she heard the hiss. She made a hasty exit and informed the members of the house.

When we entered the larder, we started searching in all possible places without any luck. Then, we spotted large bins with lids which made us suspicious. Cautiously, we opened a couple of them but without any luck. The third bin yielded the desired result. Our friend was lying happily curled up at the bottom! By the inertness of the snake and the size of its belly, we could ascertain that the fellow had had a good meal and was in no mood to attack. It was child's play to pick up the fellow and put into a cloth bag. There was no resistance offered by the cobra. Maybe it continued to sleep inside the bag.

Of course, my friend was very grateful for helping him out of the crisis. We advised him to repair the mesh of the larder and get rid of the remaining rats by some means.

3. This incident is to highlight that snakes have no emotions like gratitude and vengeance to which Indian mythology adheres to. Snakes have a primitive brain and all their actions are reflex in nature to protect them.

The road near our house was being freshly asphalted and there was a lot of noise with the machines and humans shouting hoarse. There was lot of black smoke and we were hoping that the process would be over soon. Many people in the locality knew of our love for animals and snakes. One of the men helping in the asphalting came running to us and informed that a big cobra was trapped in the wet asphalt and struggling to get out. We immediately went with our usual cloth bag and a stick. We saw that indeed an adult cobra was stuck in the sticky asphalt and had suffered a few burns due to the heat of the tar. We could not separate the cobra from the wet asphalt and picked up the reptile along with the black tar sticking to it. The cobra was naturally very angry and agitated. Handling it without getting bitten was really difficult. After bringing the struggling cobra to the house, we set about to clean the tar stuck to the snake. The snake was naturally under the impression that it was being harmed and repeatedly tried to inflict a bite. My brother held on to the head of the snake with one hand and prevented the lashing of the tail with the other. I meanwhile, got a kerosene bottle and started wiping the snake's body with a cloth dipped in dripping kerosene. The snake on its part must have thought that we are squeezing the life out of it and renewed its effort to get away. After nearly half-an-hour, which seemed like ages, we were able to get most of the black material from its body without causing much of an abrasion. We kept the cobra for a few days and then released it in the wilderness. The cobra, if it were to be really intelligent and having a reasoning mind, would not have behaved in this manner. In fact, we had given it a second lease of life by helping.

As an afterthought I would like to mention here that the elders of the family always insist not to kill a snake. It is their premise that the mate of the deceased snake will come searching for it and take revenge on the people who killed it. The scientific explanation is very conclusive. When a snake is grievously injured it lets out a scent called pheromones, which makes other snakes in the vicinity to come and investigate. This is purely a physiological response of the snake because a similar pheromone or scent is given out during the mating season, which is tracked by the opposite sex which culminates in mating and propagation of the species. A dying snake also lets out a similar scent and attracts the opposite sex. This is inferred by the people as seeking of vengeance by the partner. To prevent this many people advice to burn the body of the snake. Scientifically, you are just masking the scent of the pheromone by the smoke and fire, thereby preventing the entry of any inquisitive member of the species.

4. I am narrating this incident to highlight the agility and stealth with which snakes can move from one place to another under the very watchful eyes of the onlooker. This incident happened in Chamarajpet, Bangalore. As usual, a person came to our house to tell that a small snake, probably a cobra, had entered the house. He also said that there were three people watching the hideout of the snake and there was no way the snake could escape. We went to the house with the regular stick and a cloth bag. The three men who were supposed to be keeping watch pointed out the place where the snake was cornered in the room. They showed the cupboard under which the snake was spotted. They were sure that the snake had not moved from there as all exits were blocked and three of them were closely keeping guard. On enquiry, they said that there was no movement what so ever. We decided to slowly shift the cupboard without harming the small snake which was supposed to be under it. There was no snake under it but only lot of dirt and cob webs. As we were searching for the elusive reptile there was a scream from the nearby pooja room. A young girl had spotted some movement near the idols neatly arranged in the pooja room. The girl pointed out to the spot behind one of the deities. We slowly removed the idols from their places and sure enough our little four inch friend was lying there. Being young and energetic and new to this world, he kept raising the hood in a sweet threatening posture, ready to strike. Using so much energy to keep erect and threaten will tire a small cobra in no time. Being cold-blooded, their energy drains fast. It was a matter of seconds to whisk the cobra and drop it into the bag. Many people thought that we were fooling them by feigning the capture. Not until we took out the little fellow and showed the crowd that we had indeed caught the snake, were they satisfied.

Right under the noses of the so-called guards, the snake was able to slither away into another adjoining room. It had climbed the couple of steps in the pooja room to be in the company of the Gods. But for the little girl spotting it among the Gods, we would have returned empty handed thinking that the whole episode was a figment of someone's imagination. The snake, on its part, must have thought that it had reached its rightful place among the gods in heaven!

5. I am a doctor, an anaesthesiologist. My work requires me to be in the Operation Theatre (OT) giving anaesthesia. As everyone knows, the OT is a secluded place with utmost precaution taken to guard against infection etc. All and sundry cannot walk into the OT. Imagine, then, the presence of a five foot long cobra inside the OT of a hospital. The hospital was a big one with international repute. One of the OT boys had spotted it in the corridor of the OT and informed his senior who promptly called me on the phone to come and help manage the situation. At that time, I was working in St. John's Hospital, Bangalore. As soon as I received the word, I requested my boss to relieve me to attend to the problem. The other hospital had sent an ambulance for this purpose and I reached the place of action in double quick time. All movement in the big hospital OT had come to a standstill. A sort of emergency appeared to have been declared. I was taken to the site immediately. The staff there pointed to one of the sieves in the ground along the drainage pipes. There was a strong smell of formalin. Formalin is a disinfectant widely used in the operation theatre. Inside the opening of the sieve, I saw this little whitish colored cobra. With great caution, I removed the sieve and nudged the cobra to make a dash for liberty. Nothing happened. Then, I realised that the cobra was very stiff. It was dead. One of the boys there told me that they had poured gallons of the formalin into the drain to prevent it from harming them. No doubt, the poor creature had suffocated to death in the narrow confines of the drain.

The doctors there asked me as to how such a big snake could have entered the OT. The answer was there for all to see. I pointed to the drainage going out of the Operation theatres. It was going into a vast open area with lots of grass and shrub. The outside drainage pipes must have got damaged making it easy for the entry of rats and bandicoots into the drainage system. The entry of the predatory cobra was but a natural corollary.

6. This incident is to highlight how religious beliefs and superstitions steal a march over ground realities. There was a similar complaint of a cobra entering a house and the occupants panicking. On entering the house we saw that the whole house was a mess. We could not step in. We had to carefully watch our step and make progress. The reason was that the whole place was strewn with lots of egg and milk poured on the floor liberally. One misjudged step and you could be counting stars.

The occupant of the house was a very pious, god-fearing man. When he saw the cobra, the first thing that came to his mind was to appease the Snake God. And how? Put many eggs on the floor and pour milk at random. The Snake God will eat his fill and go away without harming any one.

One thing the common man should understand is that this myth of snakes drinking milk and eating eggs is very old. I always ask the people as to how a snake can have access to milk in the forest. Do they go and attach their mouths to lactating wild cows? Man is the only animal on earth to continue to drink milk after his infancy because he has made dairy farming possible. Snakes cannot get milk from anywhere in their natural habitat. Then, one may ask, how is it that snakes when offered milk consume it? Yes. When a thirsty snake is offered any liquid for that matter it will consume it to quench its thirst. It is like a human being who relishes a soft drink instead of plain water.

Then, what about the egg? Even though some snakes eat small bird eggs, there are only a couple of snakes which are adapted to eating big eggs as their staple diet. They are called egg eating snakes. These snakes do not have any teeth in their jaws. There is a small protrusion at the far end of the mouth. When the snake swallows the egg, it hits the hard tooth-like structure at the back of the mouth which breaks the egg. The contents of the egg go into the stomach and the white shell is spit out by the snake. The ordinary cobra is not adapted to do this and hence will show no interest in the egg.

7. Once, we were called to catch a snake which was lying curled up in the garden. The snake appeared to be in no mood to escape. It did not show any movement whatsoever on our approach. This was really strange. Then, we saw that the cobra was making some movement in its belly. In no time, we saw four frogs coming out of the mouth of the cobra. The snake had vomited the frogs in order to be agile enough to flee. This was a mechanism which made the snake light on its belly (feet) to enable it to fight or flee.

8. This incident is to highlight how presence of mind and calmness during an emergency situation can alleviate the problem. Most of us panic during an emergency and the thought process goes haywire. A trained mind will not allow such a thing to happen. A trained mind allows for sane thinking. It prioritizes the actions needed at the time.

I had come home from duty at St. John's hospital late in the afternoon. I was very hungry and about to have lunch. There was a clanging of the gate latch and a person on a bicycle was shouting "Sar, Sar!" I went out to see a person holding an adult cobra in one hand and the cycle handle in the other. He told me that he had cycled all the way from a factory where he had caught the cobra. One hand held the neck of the cobra and the other the handle bar of the cycle. He had cycled about six kilometres in this manner. I told him to wait and rushed into the house to get a cloth bag which was always kept handy.

I explained to the person as to how he has to put the snake inside the bag. I repeatedly told him not to release the grip he had on the snake till I told him. This was to ensure that the snake does not bite my finger which was holding the bag. In spite of this, the person who had the courage to catch a cobra and cycle such a distance holding on to it, panicked. In one swift movement he threw the snake into the bag. This was my undoing. The big cobra was standing erect in the bag and before I could blink, had a go at my finger. I felt one fang hitting the tip of my right ring finger and the other fang grazing the skin. After making sure that the snake was secure inside the bag, I rushed into the house and told my mother that I was bitten by the cobra. Meanwhile, I held on to the base of my ring finger tightly and asked my mother to tie a heavy thread around. This was the tourniquet to prevent further spread of the venom. Then, I went to the wash basin and nicely washed and squeezed the tip of my finger under running water.

With the help of my neighbour, I went back to St. John's hospital for further observation and treatment. I was not feeling giddy or light-headed and was fully in my senses. I knew that the venom injected was half the normal dose, because only one fang had pierced my skin. Also, I had given the best first aid possible by washing and squeezing the bitten area to reduce the venom intake. The problem, if at all, would start only after releasing the tight band of thread around the finger. The release of the tourniquet would allow whatever venom was in the tissues to enter the general circulation and cause systemic effect. This was the crucial time when intervention would be required.

The doctors at the hospital examined me. They examined my eyes and asked whether I had double vision. They took the ECG and looked for any weakness or breathlessness which was the first sign of envenomation after release of tourniquet. Nothing of the sort happened. I could feel a tingling sensation along the nerves on the outer side of my right arm. This was the venom travelling along my lymphatics. This sensation travelled up to the armpit. Then, the lymphatics would have emptied into the general circulation and I would get the effect of the venom, if at all. Except for a little weakness of the right arm and a catch in the arm pit, nothing else happened. The doctors advised me to stay overnight to observe any ill effects. By this time, it was evening and I was ravenously hungry. The doctors shifted me from casualty to the Intensive Care unit. There, they had made ready to give anti-snake venom injection to me through the fluid bottles. I flatly refused saying that without any symptoms, the injection was unnecessary and cause side effects of its own. The doctors were adamant. I told them in no uncertain terms that I would not take the injection. By now, my temper was running high because of hunger gnawing at my guts. The doctors made me sign a form which said that I was going against their medical advice. I was shifted to the ward. I ordered for something to eat and with a full stomach was able to relax. I spent the night in the ward. Being a staff of the hospital and at the same time refusing to take treatment which I felt was not required, made the other doctors feel uneasy. The next morning, the Hospital Administrator came to see me in the ward. He asked whether the night was peaceful. I said no. He thought that the snake bite must have been painful and asked as such. I told him that the newly-built special wards on the fifth floor of the hospital had no mosquito screens and that the nasty insects had a field day sucking my blood. He had a hearty laugh and immediately ordered for adequate measures to be taken. As for me, I just hung around till around 9:00 AM and went to the OT for my regular work as I had no problem. All the hospital had come to know about my little mishap and wanted to know first-hand as to what had happened. My voice grew hoarse narrating the incident repeatedly.

Here, I would like to highlight the importance of correct diagnosis of poisonous snake bite and appropriate treatment. Not all poisonous snake bites need treatment with anti-snake venom. Here was my own example. Many a time, it so happens that the patient goes with the history of snake bite without knowing whether it was poisonous or not. The doctor usually assumes it to be poisonous. There are many instances where anti-snake venom has been administered unnecessarily. One should note that the treatment itself can cause problems because of hypersensitivity to the anti-snake venom and therefore should be used judiciously under proper supervision.

9. The public had come to know that we were running a rescue and rehabilitation centre for animals and we were receiving many injured or orphaned animals. Some of the bolder members of the public would catch snakes on their own and bring it to us to rehabilitate the same.

There was a factory on the outskirts of Bangalore which was planning an expansion and was in the process of clearing the undergrowth. Since there was a thick cover of green many small animals had made it their home. Among the dwellers were snakes too. A couple of the workers who had seen our skill in catching snakes thought that they could do the same. Since the snakes they saw were quite small, measuring less than a foot in length, they started catching them on their own and put them in plastic bottles with air holes in the lid. The first batch of such snakes which came to us was identified as cat snakes since they had yellow colored eyes. These snakes are non-poisonous and seldom bite. We told the workers as such which emboldened them to catch and bring several more snakes. We were surprised that the area had more than a hundred of these creatures. But, we were in for a surprise. Not all the snakes in the subsequent catch were cat snakes. The similar looking venomous and most dangerous Saw- scaled Viper was among them. For a lay man, these deadly snakes appeared like the harmless cat snakes and they were all picked up casually by the ignorant and unassuming workers and delivered to our doorstep.

This episode reminds me of the saying 'ignorance is bliss.' Fortunately for the factory workers there was not a single casualty. It was another matter that we educated the workers later about how the cat snake and the Saw-scaled Viper resemble each other in their external markings and also how to differentiate the two. The factory was very thankful for the rehabilitation of the snakes and also profoundly grateful for the propagation of useful knowledge regarding the snakes among its workers.

10. One thing that we have appreciated over the years is that each snake has a character of its own like humans. Just like how you have aggressive people and docile people and a varied group in between, snakes also show varied temperament. Some snakes allow themselves to be handled without much of a fuss where as others are extremely touchy. Certain myths speak of heightened excitement among snakes during full moon days and associated astronomical events. Our experience shows that there is no correlation between such phases of the moon and the nervous excitement of the snakes. It is just that each snake behaves differently as they are different individuals.

11. Snakes are very resilient to external conditions as our experience shows. One such instance which comes to mind is a cobra which was cornered under the granite slabs leading into the house. A big crowd had gathered when we went there. We saw smoke emanating from under the granite slabs. Somebody had ignited a fire with old newspapers to force the snake to come out. The reptile refused to budge from its position. We told the onlookers to make way. The first thing we did was to douse the fire and look for the limbless visitor. The snake had gotten into a crevice and was pretty safe from the heat and smoke of the fire. We then had to loosen one of the granite slabs and physically poke the snake with a long stick to make it come out. Once out of the crevice, it was easy to bag it.

The other instance happened in a big house in 5th block Jayanagar. The snake was spotted on the terrace of the house. The easiest way out for the cobra was to get into the big drainage pipe opening. But instead of making an exit from the drainage pipe at the ground level, it refused to come out in the open. Buckets and buckets of water were emptied through the pipe. Nothing happened. Somebody suggested soap water. Another suggested mixing water with strong asafoetida and smashed ginger. The smell of asafoetida was very strong and made us hold our breath. The snake still refused to come out. Ultimately we suggested breaking the asbestos drainage pipe to get at the snake. Only then were we able to bag it.

12. There is myth which says that snakes do not venture into a place where a particular type of plant is grown. This plant is called Naga Dali Soppu. The plant has gotten a peculiar odour which is supposed to put off the snake. We have come across snakes happily sleeping in the shade of these plants without a care in the world.

13. Catching water snakes as said earlier is tricky. Though they are non-poisonous, they give nasty bites. Water snakes generally feed on frogs. Whenever there are frogs in the garden you could expect cobras or water snakes to come there. On many occasions on attempting to catch the Water Snake, to increase its agility and to reduce the burden of the meal in its belly, the snake vomits out the frogs. We have seen that many times, the frogs are still alive, except for a few burnt spots where the acid of the snake's stomach has acted. The frogs go about hopping in their usual way as though nothing had happened. The same does not occur with a cobra because the venom of the cobra would have killed the frog or any other animal.

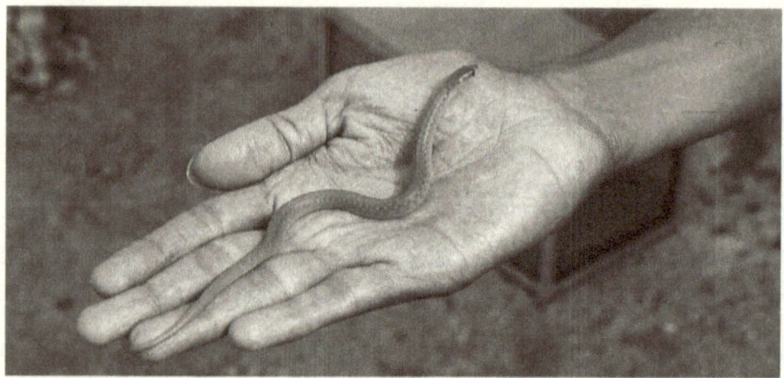

Young Water snake

Water snake eggs and young ones

14. Snakes entering the vehicles like scooters and cars are not rare. We have had snakes going into the exhaust pipe of the car in winter months to keep warm. Snakes being found inside the bonnet are also quite common. This is mainly because of the heat of the engine during cold months that the snake prefers to rest in such places.

15. When working in St. John's Hospital, as an Anaesthesiologist I was called to a place in the Hospital where lot of building material was stocked. The workers had spotted a huge snake about eight feet in length and yellow in color. I could surmise that it was a Rat Snake. This place where the snake was spotted was visible from almost all the floors of the hospital and I could see that almost all the inmates of the hospital were seeing the action which was going to unfold. I boldly ventured to search for the snake. I knew for sure that it was a Rat Snake so I need not be too careful regarding getting bitten. Such a huge snake cannot hide for too long between wooden logs. The tail was spotted and it was a matter of time before I could pull the snake out of its hiding with effort. The huge snake – one of the biggest I have caught independently – was lunging in all directions to bite and get away. During one of the lunges it caught hold of my trousers. The Rat Snake was unable to let go immediately as the backward-facing teeth could not be dislodged with ease. Releasing the bite would have been easier from the skin as it would be soft. I seized the opportunity and grabbed the portion just behind its head and slowly disengaged the teeth from my trousers without injuring the snake. This amount of excitement had caused the snake to release a lot of foul smelling gas. The stench in the area was unbearable. The next step was to put the huge fellow into a bag. I started walking towards the casualty department. I knew there were huge pillows with covers there. I told the nurse there to take out the pillow cover. One of the bolder spectators volunteered to hold the pillow cover for me to transfer the snake. Even a big pillow cover was insufficient to hold the huge Rat Snake. With a little manoeuvring I managed. I secured the pillow cover twice over as these snakes can keep poking their head near a weak point and get out in no time. I promised the nurse that I would get the pillow cover back after a good wash. The next day the whole hospital including the patients who had seen the action from all the five floors of the hospital wanted to congratulate me which I humbly accepted.

16. MOULTING- Snakes and other reptiles shed their skin periodically. Maybe this is the reason people feel that snakes are immortal. The process of shedding the skin is called "Ecdysis." This process is hormone regulated. Couple of days prior to the actual process a thin milky fluid starts accumulating under the skin along the entire body. The snake becomes lethargic and irritable. This is because the milky fluid forms over the eyes also and disturbs the vision which is very vital. After a couple of days, the snake starts rubbing its nose against some hard object which splits the skin. Once this is done, the snake again starts rubbing the sides of the body and slowly wriggles out of the old skin. The shed skin comes inside out like pulling out the stockings. The new skin is all glittering, giving the hitherto dull snake a fresh look. The snake will generally be hungry as it would not have eaten during the past three or four days. Some snakes have a problem in shedding the skin in one piece. It may come off in pieces. The problem occurs when the old skin over the eye refuses to come off. It may get stuck on to the eye on one or both sides. This causes corneal opacity and the snake will be blind in that eye. The next schedule of shedding will aggravate the problem by the accumulation of another layer of dead skin over the already blind eye. Unless physically removed by some means the snake will suffer from blindness. This periodic shedding of the skin and the subsequent look of rejuvenation could be the reason why the snake is made out to be immortal in mythology. Shed skin of snakes has no value. This is what we thought until we were proved otherwise. Many school children used to visit our premises to see and learn a few things about the snakes and other animals we had. Once, one of the boys, after being shown how shed skin looked, asked whether he could have a piece of it. Our curiosity was piqued and we wanted to know the reason. Somebody at home had told him that if he could acquire a piece of the shed skin of a snake and keep it inside the text book of a subject he was weak in, he would pass. This was news to us. The boy was really under the impression that his memory in the subject would improve. Imagine if such things were true every one having an access to shed skin would be in the elite Mensa club along with the likes of Einstein and Ramanujams. The periodicity of the process of skin shedding varies depending on the activity of the snake and its age. Growing young snakes naturally shed more often to accommodate their growing bodies.

17. To tell the sex of the snake is difficult, unless there is sexual dimorphism. Rat Snakes, cobras, water snakes etc. do not have any difference externally to distinguish between male and female. The Green Vine Snake also called the Long-nosed tree snake is one snake where the female is heavily built and long. The male is very short and thin.

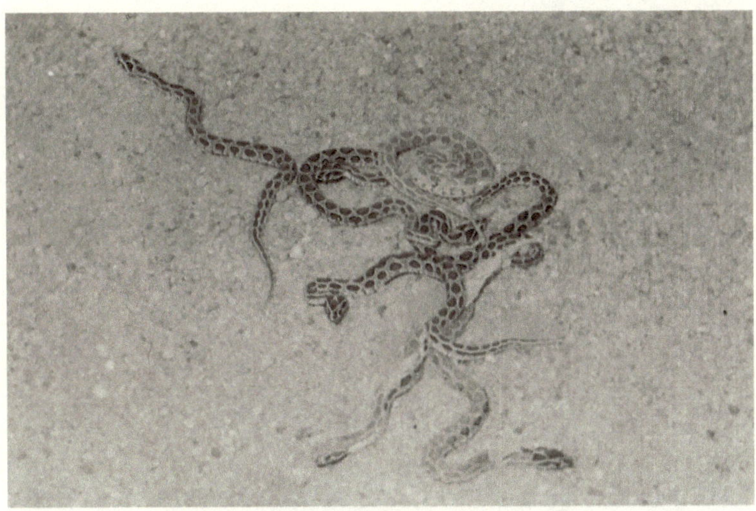

Russell's viper young ones in ecdysis

The only way to tell the sex in the other snakes is to do a cloacal examination. Introducing a sterile blunt tipped metal probe into the cloaca is conclusive. If the probe stops short without going in deep, it means it is a male and otherwise a female. Males of all snakes have a bifid penis (double). Also it is to be noted that mating cannot occur between different species of snakes. Many people are of the belief that the cobra and Rat Snakes are of opposite sex and capable of mating. This is not true. There are many things regarding snakes which would be of interest for the lay man.

The Green Vine Snake is quite common in gardens. This snake is thin and long with a pointed nose at the tip. On inflating its body, the green color changes. Black checks appear in between the green markings and the snake looks scary. Added to this the snake takes a lunge at the intruder. Since the snake is at the eye level of the human, it is but natural to think that the green snake is attacking the eyeball of the victim. Added to this the eyeball of the snake is horizontal with a horizontal pupil. This is for it to perceive any movement of lizards among the greenery. All arboreal (tree dwelling) snakes have similar shaped eyeballs. Another use to which the snake is put is to clean the inside of the human ear. The tame Vine Snake is held by the snake charmer and the tail is put inside the ear of the customer. The tail keeps wriggling and gives a pleasant sensation to the customer. The ear is supposed to be cleaned in this manner. This was a very common sight in bus stations and railway stations before the wild life act laws came into force.

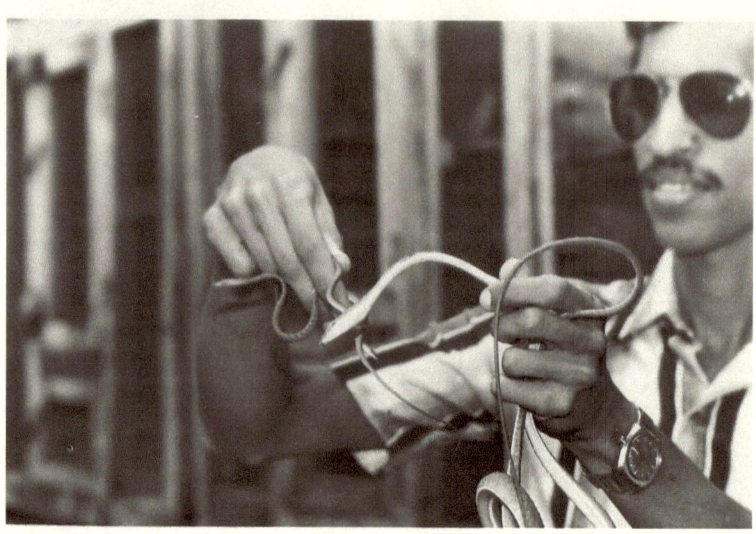

Vine snake

18. Hitherto I have not mentioned anything about the Russell's Viper. This is one of the most-feared snakes even among professional snake catchers. This is because it is highly evolved and always bites effectively. This snake can lunge backwards and is very fast. Unlike a cobra where you can plant a kiss on its nose by diverting its attention elsewhere, the viper is very sensitive. Even an approach from the back is dangerous, as it can sense your presence. It is difficult to pin down a viper as easily as a cobra. The fangs are very long and kept folded along the side of the jaw like a foldable knife. The best way to catch as far as I know is to use a little longer stick and just pick up the snake on it and transfer the snake into a bag kept on the ground with the mouth open. Better not to involve any one else in holding the bag.

19. Many times, it has so happened that the snake which we had caught in the wild would be pregnant and would lay eggs in the enclosure or would deliver young snakes. Let me explain. There are two types of snakes – one which lays eggs (Oviparous) and another which gives birth to young ones (Viviparous). Cobras, pythons, water snakes and Rat Snakes lay eggs which will hatch in about two months' time. Vipers are the only group which bears live young ones. We have had water snakes, Rat Snakes etc laying eggs and subsequently hatching, provided the conditions outside were favourable. We have a couple of instances where Russell's Vipers have delivered twenty or thirty young ones. The poisonous snakes have poison at birth, whether they come through the egg or straight away. The quantity of venom is small but nevertheless effective.

Russell's viper with young

Green Keelback laying eggs

Nowadays, a snake snaring device is available even on the internet which can be safely used without any harm to the snake and also the handler. Things are definitely easier and better now when compared to thirty years ago. Some snakes do not get accustomed to handling where as some species like the Trinket Snake and Striped Keelback behave as though they have been with us for a long time. Hence, these snakes are called gentleman snakes because they seldom bite even when encountered in the wild.

Trinket snake

SAND BOA

Sand Boas are cousins of the python and anaconda. There are two types of Sand Boas. They grow hardly two feet in length. One of them is reddish brown in color. They burrow by nature, and hence their eyes are very small and rudimentary. They dig the sand or mud and keep their tails and heads a little above the mud. The most peculiar thing about this red Sand Boa is that it has a blunt tail unlike most of the other snakes. This tail is kept wriggling on the surface. Any prey like a rat will come close to satisfy its curiosity. The snake will wait for such a moment. Without wasting any time, it will throw its coils around the prey and squeeze the life out of it. This is a mechanism of hunting by stealth and trickery adopted by this particular species. Many snake charmers make people believe that this snake has two heads. People also spread stories that the head changes ends every six months. Hence, it is popularly called two-headed snake. The snake looks like a gigantic earthworm.

There is another Sand Boa which is also commonly seen in India. It is called the conical Sand Boa or Russell's Boa. This is because the marking on it resembles that of a Russell's Viper. This is called animal mimicry, where a non-poisonous snake to safeguard itself from predators, masquerades as a poisonous one. In fact, we have seen many instances where people with snake bites thought they were bitten by the viper, but when asked to identify, they have picked on the boa. Unlike the red boa this snake has a very pointed and conical tail, hence the name. This snake does not bury itself in the sand. One very peculiar phenomenon occurs with these conical Sand Boas in captivity. Some of these snakes refuse to feed on anything during captivity. It is difficult to force feed them. Over a period of time their jaws refuse to open apart and some sort of an adhesion occurs with a sticky substance in between. Some people refer to this as mouth rot. We are not sure. The same snake, when released in the wild becomes normal and starts hunting its prey, as though nothing had happened. In this manner, one Sand Boa did not eat anything for more than a year and a half. But for a little loss of weight the snake looked quite healthy. Maybe this is a record of some sort.

Russell's Boa

SNAKE VENOM

Poisonous snakes produce small quantities of venom which is milked periodically. This venom is very precious for the snake to survive. The venom literally is equal to its weight in gold. Venom is used in manufacture of many drugs. Viper venom is used on people with blood clotting disorders. The cobra and krait venom is used as an ingredient in pain killers used in cancer. The method of milking a snake is quite simple if handled with care and caution. A glass container with a thin rubber membrane tied to the mouth is taken. The snake to be milked is held firmly by the handler behind the head with one hand. The snake is made to bite the rubber sheet on the tumbler by opening its mouth and gently pressing on either side of the upper jaw where the glands are located. A few drops of golden colored liquid come out. This is collected in the glass. The liquid, after some time, solidifies to crystals. The potency of this solid crystal remains, eternally. If by chance a person rubs this crystal into an open wound, the venom gets absorbed into the system and the effect is the same as a poisonous snake bite.

Many people believe that ingesting the venom through the mouth is also poisonous. This is not so because the venom is a mixture of various proteins and gets digested. The problem occurs if the person were to have a bleeding ulcer in the mouth or in the stomach. Then, the venom gets a straight entry into the blood stream and can cause toxic effects.

Many people bitten by a snake are given unnecessary treatment with antivenin medicine. Our experience and that of scientific papers say that statistically seven out of ten bites are caused by non-venomous snakes where there is no need to give an antidote. Here, only preventive tetanus injection and thorough cleaning of the wound in running water is enough. Even among the cobra bites, not all bites are fateful. Many factors are important in the amount of venom entering the body of the victim. A very young snake will have less venom than an adult. Whether the snake was able to get either fangs in or just one (as in my case). The quantity of venom is naturally halved with only one fang. The presence of intervening clothing and its thickness matters. A thick fabric like a denim jeans will go a long way in reducing the effectiveness of the bite. The area bitten is also of significance. If it a bony surface like the ankle, not much venom can go in. The same is not true with fleshy areas like the calf muscles in the back of the leg. An old snake or a diseased snake may not produce good quantity of venom. Pigs which have a lot of fat hardly get affected because of the venom not able to get into the blood stream. This is because fat has very little blood supply.

There is a vast difference in the mechanism of the cobra and the viper bites. The cobra is not as highly evolved as a viper. The cobra has a fang which is open on one side like the gutter. The viper has a fang which is like a hypodermic needle used in injections by the doctor. The cobra cannot give an effective bite whereas the viper is sure to get all the venom in. Moreover, the viper has fangs which are three times longer than that of a cobra. Hence, its penetration is deep. The viper fang is not seen because it is kept folded in the jaw like a pocket knife.

It is better to have some knowledge regarding the venom of the cobra and the viper. They act in different ways and on different organs of the body. Cobra venom is mainly neurotoxic and causes paralysis. When the respiratory muscles get affected there is breathing difficulty and the person or animal dies due to inadequate oxygen. This can be prevented by giving artificial respiration and suitable drugs to reverse the paralysis. The viper venom is mainly haemotoxic. It causes disruption in the blood clotting mechanism. There is internal bleeding which is the cause of death. This effect can also be reversed to a certain extent by modern drugs which allow clotting to occur. But, the problem is that the local effect of the viper venom causes a lot of damage to the tissues. This is called necrosis and the tissue will have to be surgically removed. Hence, the viper bite apart from being more effective is also more damaging to the tissues.

KING COBRA

The King Cobra as the name indicates is really a king among the snakes. The sheer length of twelve or fifteen feet is enough to scare the wits out of the hapless victim whether human or animal. Added to this, the venom quantity is very huge. Even if the antivenin is available at hand, large doses are required to neutralise the venom. The venom is neurotoxic as in the common cobra.

King cobra

The King Cobra specialises in devouring other snakes. The staple diet for the King Cobra is the Rat Snake. Other snakes like the Water Snake are also preyed upon. We had the opportunity to house the King Cobra for a few months before giving it to the Reptile Park at Bannerghatta. Great care is to be exercised while catching or transferring the huge snake. The King Cobra's hiss is very long and is more of a grunt because of its low pitch when compared to the common cobra. One method of disarming the King Cobra was taught to us by our old friend Khasim. A big piece of cloth is first thrown into the enclosure. The cloth is aimed at the head of the King Cobra. The snake instinctively reacts by biting into the cloth. Once the snake realises that it is not palatable, it tries to spit the cloth. This takes time as the backward-pointing teeth are structured to hold on to the prey. During this time, one is supposed to pin down the snake which is relatively harmless and transfer it to another enclosure.

Another major problem for the King Cobra was to provide them with live Rat Snakes. This was next to impossible and hence the early release in the park.

There are some snakes like the Green Vine Snake which also have venom. But this venom comes from the teeth in the back of the mouth. The Vine Snake after catching the prey moves it to the back of the mouth where this poison comes into action. This venom is not as powerful as that of the cobra and viper. It is meant to paralyse small prey which keeps struggling.

The last point I would like to share with the readers regarding the snakes is that some species of snakes are moody. Pythons are moody snakes. What exactly does it mean? You might have observed that your pet dog many a time will not be in a mood to play or may insist on playing when you are not in the mood. The dog can express itself by various means to its master and by the mere body language one can find out. Among snakes this is not possible. Pet snakes on repeated handling may not like it. How does it convey that it does not like being touched? By sudden lunging and biting. This is most commonly seen among the bigger and heavier snakes to which the python belongs. Our pet python had done this on a number of occasions. We have not observed such behaviour among other snakes.

Python

MALAYSIAN TREE SNAKE

A very unique way of how snakes cross countries should be noted here. A timber merchant who used to import big logs of wood from other countries had a problem. A load of timber from Malaysia had been unloaded in his factory. One of the workers, when processing the wood, noticed a bunch of eggs in the cavity of the huge log of wood. He immediately contacted his boss and within no time the owner was at our place with the log containing the eggs. We took the eggs into our care. Twenty days later we were surprised to see young snakes emerging from the eggs. About eight slender green snakes emerged from the eggs. We later identified them as the Malaysian Tree Snake since the log had come from there. The snakes resembled our Vine Snake. They were released in an appropriate habitat.

TYPHLOPS

Typhlops are also called blind snakes. They are burrowing snakes, are small and look like earthworms. They are among the smallest snakes in the world. They have no need for eyes, as they are underground most of the time. Unlike the earthworms, typhlops do not have rings on their bodies.

Typhlops

WOLF SNAKES

Wolf snakes are black in color with white cross bands which resemble the pattern of the banded krait. Animal mimicry is at play here. The wolf snake, by projecting itself as a poisonous snake, protects itself by imitating the coloration of the Banded Krait.

Wolf snake

OTHER REPTILES

CROCODILE

Would anyone like to have a six foot long crocodile as a pet? Feed it and pet it? Sounds scary and crazy? But, believe it or not, we had one. The story (rather, fact) goes like this. One day, we got a call from Indiranagar from a fish merchant. He said that among the lot of fish which was delivered by the fishermen, there was this small one foot long baby crocodile. It was alive and well with no injuries. Would we be interested to take care of the croc? Why not? It would be a new and thrilling experience. We set out at once to get the scaly young monster. The fish merchant had kept it in a plastic tub. It was not aggressive. It looked very pretty and cute. Being immobile for hours together was its habit. It looked like a model. We just picked the fellow in our hands, put him (or her) in a cloth bag and brought it home. We put the croc in a tub with a little water and some sand on one side. It could either go into the water or stay on the sand. Another very important requirement for all cold-blooded animals was sunlight. Without getting warm in the sun, these creatures would not be able to muster enough energy to move around and hunt. Morning sunlight was very crucial for the survival of the young ones. The croc did not eat anything for the first two days. Then, we decided to force feed with minced meat. One of us would hold the neck of the croc and try to open the mouth, while another would be ready with a small piece of meat to push inside the mouth. After a couple of meat pieces went in, the croc hopefully would realise that it was food to be eaten and attempt to eat on its own. For the sake of information, Crocodiles have a tongue but cannot move it like the snake or other mammals as it is fixed to the base of the mouth. Hence, after biting into the carcass, the crocodile has to turn its whole body to dislodge the bitten piece from the carcass.

Like snakes, which do not eat every day, the croc would get hungry once in two or three days and a few pieces of meat was sufficient for its needs. Within a couple of weeks, we realised that the croc had grown and the container of water was too small for it. We had to get a bigger tub and the enclosure had to be bigger. It is a well-known fact that the crocodile keeps growing in proportion to the water body in which it dwells. If a croc were to be in small pond, the growth would be restricted when compared to the same being in a big lake. It is well-known that crocs keep growing as they are shifted to bigger and bigger bodies of water. This way, with good timely food, sunlight and big space our croc grew to a length of more than six feet in a matter of few months.

Even though the croc was harmless, handling it would be a problem. We realised that we could not provide a bigger space for it in the days to come. It would be injustice on our part in not allowing the croc to grow to its full potential. Hence, we decided to rehabilitate the croc at the BNP. Arrangements were made to translocate it to better surroundings.

In the bargain, we had gleamed valuable first-hand information about the behaviour and growth of the crocodile.

CHAMELEON

Chameleons are peculiar lizards. Unlike other lizards which are fast moving, Chameleons are very slow moving. Everyone knows how chameleons change color and camouflage themselves among the foliage. It is very difficult to spot them among the greenery. We have had the opportunity to keep them as pets. We have had about ten to twelve of them at different times in the last thirty to forty years. The first experience with a chameleon was when my father brought one home about fifty years ago. Being a mining engineer he had to walk long distances in wooded areas and once he came across a specimen and brought it home. Of course, he had read a lot about chameleons and their harmless nature and their diet etc. My father had told that chameleons have a very long and sticky tongue which is longer than the length of the chameleon and is shot at a cockroach or grasshopper at great speed. The prey gets stuck to the tongue and within a fraction of a second the tongue is back inside the mouth with the prey. We also knew that chameleons are adept in changing their skin color and also the shape of their body.

We saw these things in practice. Being caught from the wild and not accustomed to human presence, the chameleon would open its mouth in a fearsome manner to threaten. The whole manoeuvre was harmless but was scary enough for other predators in the forest. The change in color was very dramatic: from light green, to dark green, to yellow and to orange and red. It was amazing. We realised that the change in color was due to its mood, the ambient light and not necessarily to its surrounding color as is most often attributed. This color change is brought about by hormones which make the different colored pigments in the skin move to the surface as required.

What were we to feed the chameleon? Cockroaches, of course! It is not difficult to get a couple of cockroaches and put them in the enclosure with the chameleon. The space available for the chameleon should be sufficient to aim and shoot its tongue at the prey. After a day of captivity, the chameleon was hungry. The moment a couple of the roaches were put in the enclosure, the chameleon focussed both its eyes on the target and with lightning speed shot the sticky tongue at the prey. Before we could blink our eyes the prey was in the mouth of the chameleon. It took a minute or so for the chewing to be complete before it was swallowed.

For people who have not seen a chameleon, it looks very strange. It moves on a twig very slowly with side to side movement to simulate a leaf gently swaying in the breeze. All the four feet have grasping toes – two on either side, unlike the house lizard. The eyes are capable of independent movement such that the left eye could be looking at the sky while the right would be focussed on the ground. Only while focussing on the prey and before shooting the tongue, do both the eyes converge.

Chameleons do drink water in a peculiar way by dipping their mouth in the water with the mouth partially open. They are difficult to keep in captivity because of difficulty in procuring so many cockroaches or other insects. It is better to rehabilitate them in the same area where they were found. Many people are of the opinion that the saliva of the chameleon is poisonous when mixed with food. This is one reason why they are exploited. The poor creature is supposed to be hung upside down with the saliva dripping out of its mouth. This saliva is collected in a receptacle and later used to poison the human enemies without leaving a trace of the murder.

MONITOR LIZARD

Monitor lizards are huge lizards compared to the house lizard. There are two varieties. One is the Land Monitor and the other Water Monitor. Water monitors are nearly five feet in length unlike their land cousins who are about two to three feet. We have had land monitors in our menagerie of different ages and sizes. The smallest and the cutest were just about a foot in length. Monitors have split tongue like the snakes. They too have a Jacobson's organ for detecting prey and sensing the environment like the snakes. Monitors have four legs and a heavy tail which is used as a whip to lash out at their rivals. Monitor lizards can be tamed with continuous handling so that they do not lash out with their tail and cause injury. They can be trained to eat meat pieces with roughage. The normal diet of the monitor lizard consists of smaller garden lizards. Water should be provided for them. Plenty of sunlight is also required because they are cold-blooded animals and need to bask in the sun to gain energy.

Monitor Lizard

Monitor lizards figure in the history text books also. Surprised? Well, they are supposed to have assisted soldiers in climbing forts and gain entry into the enemy stronghold. The monitor lizard is supposed to have a phenomenal grip in its feet and not supposed to let go, come what may. The soldiers were supposed to tie a thick rope to the waist of the lizard and throw it high up on to the wall of the fort. The lizard was supposed to hold on to the crevices in the fort wall. With the rope dangling from the waist, the soldiers were supposed to climb the fort wall easily, one after another. But, the fact is that the poor lizard does not have such a grip. It is not like the house lizard, the gecko, which can climb the walls and the roof of our houses. It does not have the suction pads like the gecko. The whole story is a myth. One possibility is that the lizard could have been left on the wall with the rope. The natural tendency of the monitor is to keep climbing up and up. During this process, the rope could have gotten entangled in some sort of a projection of stone etc. This could have given the soldiers the chance to climb the rope.

SPINY TAILED LIZARD

These are small lizards measuring six to eight inches. These lizards are harmless but have a set of spines on their back to look formidable. They are greyish in color. They are found in the desert regions of north India. They are caught in groups and sold all over India illegally. People believe that the oil extracted from the lizard is effective against joint pains. To prevent the lizard from running away, their backs are broken causing paralysis in the hind legs. It is a pitiable sight. Such confiscated lizards have been brought to our centre.

In captivity, they hardly eat or drink. It is but a slow death for them. We have to force a few drops of water into their mouths. In the wild, they are herbivorous, subsisting on flowers and leaves of plants. In captivity, we have not seen them eat anything. Some of the lizards which have survived for long after their back injury show a bulge at the point of injury due to extra and irregular bone growth.

Apart from the spiny tailed lizard which is hunted for its oil, snakes and monitor lizards are also targeted for this. In fact, at one time about twenty-five years ago, there were lot of foreign students studying in India. They were mainly from Iran and Iraq. They were the customers for the oil. In broken English they would ask for snake oil. The snake charmers would make a killing by demanding exorbitant amounts for the oil. There was a fall in demand when the Iran-Iraq war took place when most of these students went back to their countries.

Spiny tailed lizard

TURTLES AND TORTOISES

Tortoises are land dwelling and do not require water to live in. They hardly drink water and make do with the water content in the vegetable matter they consume. Turtles live in water and they can be fresh water or salt water depending on the species. We had both types under our care. Both the varieties had gotten used to eating rice mixed with curd. It had become a habit for all of them to eagerly anticipate the curd rice in the afternoon at the time we finished lunch. They were free to roam in the backyard and would wait patiently at the threshold for their quota. The turtles had laid about eight eggs which we had preserved in sand kept in a basket. Imagine our surprise when two months down the line they all hatched and had to be rehabilitated at the appropriate time. Now let us move on to the other animals which have passed through our ARRT.

Soft shell turtle

Star tortoise

BLACK SCORPION

What? A scorpion, as a pet? One must be crazy. Well it was not our intention to have a scorpion as a pet, but to observe its behaviour. What prompted us to keep a scorpion was again our old friend, Khasim. These snake charmers were adept in taming the fiery scorpion. We wanted to know how he accomplished such a dangerous feat. Having been with us for a long time, Khasim

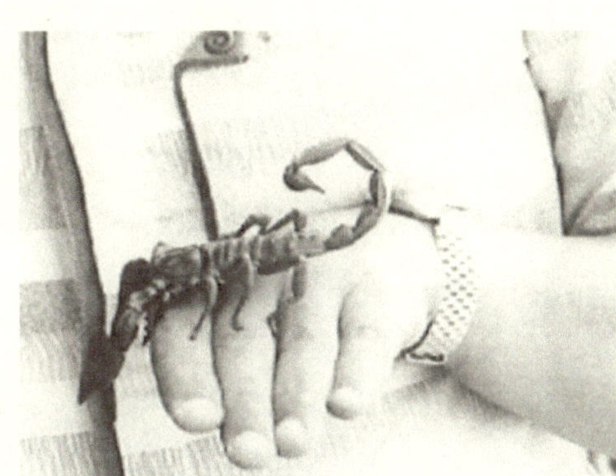

Black Scorpion

revealed the secret. The sting which is at the tip of the segmented tail is made blunt and relatively ineffective. This literally takes the sting out of the sting. The scorpion meanwhile is able to catch hold of its prey like the cockroach or house cricket with its huge front legs which act like pincers. After some time, the scorpion mends the sting and makes it effective.

Black Scorpion

One such black scorpion happened to be a female. We were ignorant that the mother gives birth to twenty to twenty-five young ones which she carries on her back till the young ones grow in size and get off her back to be independent.

MAMMALS

JACKAL

Let me start with the jackal. The jackal is a very cunning animal, being a cousin of the fox. The first jackal which came to us as a cub of about four months stayed with us for a long time. We named her Dheeru – meaning brave. This was a misnomer. The jackal, even though cunning, was extremely timid. Dheeru had company in the form of four dogs. We had with us at that time three Cocker Spaniels and a Pomeranian spitz. We thought that being in the company of the dogs and intermingling with us through the dogs would enable the jackal to overcome its timidity. No such luck. Dheeru marginally improved over a period of years in overcoming this fear.

Once she grew up, we would try to take her out for a walk along with the other canine friends. Dheeru would play a little with other dogs but the dogs preferred to play among themselves rather than involve the alien. This way Dheeru was isolated. There was a small kennel in the front passage of our house where we had tied Dheeru. She was comfortable living in the kennel with freedom to roam about freely twice a day. Dheeru had the same diet as of our pet dogs.

Dheeru-Jackal

EXPLOITS OF DHEERU

Once, we had to shift our residence along with all the animals. It was a tedious process. The household things had all been shifted. The animals in cages like the birds and other small mammals were also shifted. We had planned to shift Dheeru at the end. Dheeru was tame enough to be handled and thus came to the new premises. We tied Dheeru with the chain at the gate since its kennel was not ready. The new neighbourhood children were very curious to know what animals were there. Seeing the jackal at the gate the children were making a big noise. This new environment was not welcomed by Dheeru and she became restless. She started pacing up and down. When we were inside the house Dheeru somehow managed to escape. The chain was off and with the collar around the neck Dheeru ran wildly. The children at the gate alerted us about the escape.

The new premises were at the outskirts of the city with a lot of wilderness around. The surroundings were like a small forest with thick undergrowth. We spotted Dheeru at a distance and called out. Even though Dheeru heard us, she played deaf and started running away. When we started chasing, Dheeru entered the thick bushes and we could see that she had covered a long distance. There was no way we could lure her back. We assumed that she would not return because she had gained freedom and also the habitat was well suited for a jackal to survive.

We returned to our new home very tired after all the excitement and chase. Dheeru was at least two or three kilometres away. We were trying to get our breath back and drinking water when we heard the children outside shouting. We wondered what the excitement was about. The children then pointed to Dheeru who was trying to get back into the house through the gate. Our joy knew no bounds. At the same time we were totally surprised at Dheeru's behaviour. We had least expected her to come back. There are many reasons for this. Dheeru, we thought was not attached to us like our pet dogs. Having escaped into her own type of habitat we thought she would be comfortable. Retracing her path in an unfamiliar surrounding was not expected. A dog leaves a trail behind by urinating. Dheeru had not done so. The only scent by which Dheeru would have retraced her steps was to smell her sweat from the paws, left on the ground. This was a remarkable feat. One important conclusion we can draw here is that even wild animals, when given good care and affection, reciprocate. It showed that Dheeru was attached to us and could not survive without us. She was like a pet dog without her master. The bonding was a strong one which compelled the jackal to retrace its steps. After the return, our affection for Dheeru increased several fold. I am sure it was the same for Dheeru also.

DHEERU AT THE FARM HOUSE

We decided to move into a farm house off the city outskirts to have more space for our animals and to give them natural habitat. Dheeru accompanied us to our new home along with other pets. Whenever the surrounding was unfamiliar, the natural instinct in Dheeru to get back to her original home would surface. This time also it was not any different. One thing which became very clear over the years by our experience was that Dheeru could somehow manage to get out of the collar if she decided to. Otherwise she was happy being chained to one place.

Dheeru in the wild

This time with the unfamiliar surroundings she decided to get free. In the night she was happily roaming free, exploring the new terrain. There were quite a few poultry farms in the vicinity and Dheeru got interested in the birds. The inherent predatory instinct surfaced and she decided to kill a few birds and eat one or two of them.

In the morning we realised that Dheeru was free and running near the new farmhouse. We offered her morning milk which she drank with relish. But, she refused to come near and get chained. We thought Dheeru would get tired running free and come to us later. Without a second thought we allowed her to be free for another night. Dheeru's palate had been tickled and she wanted some more fat chicken. Again she went on a hunting spree killing several birds.

Next morning the people in the locality had come to know that our jackal was loose and also knew who had plundered their poultry farm. We saw four or five of the villagers coming to us asking for compensation and to get rid of the culprit.

We had no other alternative but to get Dheeru chained at the earliest. That day till evening we tried to lure Dheeru inside the house with all sort of temptations. Dheeru had gotten wise when it came to the trick and refused to be conned. We did not wish the wrath of the poultry people. We had to do something fast before the night to secure Dheeru.

We had come to the conclusion that we could not chain Dheeru with tricks or treat. We hit upon the idea of putting some sleeping pills in the milk and feed Dheeru the same. On being sedated it would be easy to catch a drowsy Dheeru. We wanted to put the plan into action without delay. We put four tablets of Calmpose (a sedative) – enough to put an adult in deep slumber. We mixed it in milk and Dheeru drank it without suspecting any foul play. We kept track of Dheeru till it became dark. We imagined that her movements were slow and her gait was altered. We expected Dheeru to be knocked out cold with the drug in the morning. But, to our dismay the poultry farms were again raided in the night and the morning brought people with their complaints.

Dheeru was her normal self in the morning without a trace of any drug effect. We decided to give a very large dose of the sedatives even if it proved lethal. We put sixteen tablets of Calmpose and six tablets of Stemetil in the milk. We saw Dheeru drink the whole milk with the drugs. We expected the drug to take effect within a couple of hours and were prepared for any eventuality. We waited till evening, but in vain. Nothing happened. The drug did not touch Dheeru. We decided to catch her by force before the night set in.

One thing with all animals is that they have a sixth sense by which they can read our thoughts. They know whether our intentions are good or bad or we mean any harm to them. In this manner, Dheeru could always follow our thought. When we walked around with some other purpose in mind Dheeru would come quite close to us. But whenever we had the intention of catching Dheeru she would keep a safe distance.

To overcome this problem we should have a blank mind which is impossible. The other thing would be to forcibly think of something else and be ready to catch Dheeru. This is what I did. I just walked near the enclosures of the animals, feeding them and talking to them. The thought of Dheeru at my heels was not there. I had to forcible blank out catching Dheeru. In my subconscious mind I knew Dheeru was very closely following me by the side. In one swift movement I fell forward and caught hold of Dheeru's front leg. Dheeru, who had not anticipated this sudden movement, was entirely taken by surprise. This frightened Dheeru and she bit me. But by then, I had taken Dheeru in both hands and was trying to allay her fears. The next moment we had a collar and chain around her.

One may ask why the drug had no effect on Dheeru. It was because the digestive system of all the canines to which Dheeru belongs is very sensitive. Any toxic material entering the system activates the vomiting centre in the brain and the animal regurgitates the toxin before any harm is done. Dheeru must have vomited the milk without our knowledge.

DHEERU AND TIPPU

Tippu was a male jackal which came to us as an adolescent. He was pretty tame. He allowed us to touch and caress him. Unlike Dheeru who was still timid, Tippu was very bold. For reason of safety we made a place for Tippu in the backyard near the bathroom and did not allow him to be close to Dheeru. After a week or so, things were going on smoothly with Tippu getting friendlier and accustomed to the new place.

Trouble started one morning at around 6:00 AM. My father while going to the bathroom in the morning was surprised at the sudden attack by Tippu. It was nothing major. Tippu nicked my father's foot for no apparent reason. There was a little bleeding and first aid was applied. After some time, my mother while going to the bathroom had a similar experience. I was called to see what the problem could be. Was something irritating Tippu? Sudden change in behaviour in an animal usually is a symptom of the dreaded RABIES. Was the new comer Tippu showing signs of RABIES? Then, it was very serious. I too got a small bite on the foot in the process. Three members were bitten. We decided to call a Veterinary doctor.

In the next couple of hours before the Vet came, we saw that Tippu was really behaving very oddly. He was going around in circles looking at the sky in the back yard. He was trying to overturn the vessel when offered food. He was trying to bite the cloth on which he was sleeping. One look at Tippu and the Vet said it was rabies. He asked us to somehow take Tippu to the Veterinary College at Hebbal where they would put the animal to sleep and then, take the brain for examination to prove the diagnosis.

I felt very sorry for Tippu. On enquiry at the St. John's Hospital where I was working, all the doctors were of the unanimous opinion regarding anti-rabies treatment for the three of us bitten by Tippu. Fortunately the new type of rabies vaccine was available which did not entail a long course of injections. I was really concerned not only for the human members, but also for Tippu. My intuition was telling me that Tippu was not rabid. But how do you account for his behaviour? How about the treatment for all of us bitten by Tippu? As you might know, rabies is one disease where there is no treatment. It has 100% mortality. Only prevention is possible by timely injections of rabies vaccine.

I started thinking as to what could have caused the change in behaviour of Tippu who was so well behaved. Could it be that the disease was in the incubatory phase till now and manifesting itself now after so many weeks?

Then, as I was standing near the gate I was watching Dheeru near her kennel. Dheeru kept on grooming herself more than usual. Then, I saw that the floor near the kennel near Dheeru was having slimy spots with blood. I went near to check what was happening. Then, I realised that Dheeru had come to heat (oestrus). Dheeru had matured. She was ready to mate. This was her first cycle. I suddenly realised that the peculiar behaviour of Tippu was because Dheeru was sending signals to Tippu through her pheromones in the atmosphere. Tippu though not able to see Dheeru was excited sexually by smelling her from a distance. Knowing that there is a female of the species nearby and that too in heat made Tippu all the more furious. The urge to mate is so strong among animals that any obstacle in this regard will make them go mad. This going around in circles, refusal of food and biting were all part of the behavioural patterns in this regard. Then, I took a bold decision. Tippu was neither going anywhere, nor were we getting any vaccination for rabies. A tetanus shot for all of us was all that was required. I knew that the pheromone stimulus from Dheeru would subside in a couple of days and Tippu would be normal. Sure enough things came back to normal in three days' time and everything was hunky dory.

Jackal with rectal prolapse: A pair of jackal cubs was brought by some villagers. They said that the mother had abandoned the cubs and was not seen for couple of days. The cubs looked quite healthy and well fed. They were quite timid like all other jackals. They were left free in the backyard. After some time, we offered milk and few pieces of meat which they ate without any problem. We had to monitor whether both of them were getting equal share of the food. It so happens that the dominant cub will prevent the junior from eating. If this is not noticed for a week or so, the weaker cub will slowly start losing weight and die due to malnutrition. It is better to feed the cubs separately so that each cub's nutrition can be monitored. We named them Kollu and Dheeru. Kollu was more aggressive of the two.

In spite of all the care given, Kollu started having problem. Three to four months down the line, Kollu started eating less and having digestion problems. At the same time we noticed that there was a small swelling on the anus. Over a week to ten days later there was a huge bulge of the anus. My friend who is a surgeon was called in to see the jackal. I knew that it was a case of rectal prolapse and needed surgical intervention. The support for the rectum was inadequate due to lax perineal muscles and any straining of the abdomen would push the rectum inside out to the exterior. My surgeon friend Dr Lakshman said that he could treat it if somebody could restrain the jackal. Kollu somehow knew that we were doing something good for him. I held Kollu firmly at the neck so that he could not turn around and bite. Dr Lakshman asked for a hot water towel. He then compressed the protruding rectum systematically to make it go back into the body. But, this was not enough. The rectum would prolapse once again on straining. For this a figure of eight stitch had to be applied to the opening of the anus which would prevent the recurrence. My friend wanted to inject some local anaesthetic at the site of the needle pricks. I pointed out that instead of pricking with local anaesthetic and again with the stitch, the jackal would not mind a direct prick with the stitch. Kollu cooperated so well, as though he was reading our thoughts. I have earlier mentioned that animals, whether pets or wild, can follow our thoughts. This was very evident in this case.

Even though the swelling at the anus subsided, Kollu was not totally alright. There was some internal problem which we could not diagnose. Over a period of time Kollu became weak and ultimately died. His sibling did not show any problem and was rehabilitated at the herbivore safari of BNP.

DOGS

Hitherto I have been talking of wild animals and their behaviour and eccentricities. Now let me discuss the various antics of the dogs that had been with us over the years. Over the years we have had Labradors, Golden Retriever, Cocker Spaniels, Pomeranians, Irish setter, Daschund, Basset hound, German shepherd, Collie, Lhasa Apso, etc. Rover, the male Pomeranian was very aggressive and would bite us at the smallest provocation. We had to be careful the way we talked and behaved with Rover. Rover was very good in his looks. Many Pomeranians have a pink or black ring under their eyes which spoils the look. Rover had no such ring and his eyes were very attractive.

Rover came to us when he was a year old and was not friendly with us. My father was an exception and he was the only member of the family who could boldly interact with Rover. We too handled him, but with a bit of fear. All dogs love to be taken for a walk and Rover was no exception. The moment he heard the sound of the metal leash, he would jump up and down and start barking in excitement. He would then come near us and wait for the leash to be clipped on his collar. He would keep tugging and we had to run to keep pace with him for the first few minutes. Later he would calm down. The rest of the walk and return back home would be uneventful. The problem would start when we had to disengage the leash from the collar. Rover would be expecting more time at the walk. This would make him very irritable. He would snap at us while removing the chain and many times has drawn blood also. We would all be very careful and weary at this moment. We would try all tricks to keep his mind away and disengage the chain. But, Rover would surely repent for this behaviour. Whenever he snapped at us, Rover would immediately go to a corner and sulk. It was very obvious that he was feeling bad. Rover would make repeated swallowing movements and put out his tongue repeatedly. We had to comfort him with nice words and say it was ok. After about half-an-hour or so, Rover would become normal and start moving around.

Once Rover developed urinary tract infection and had to be hospitalised. Rover would sleep on the floor with his forelimbs extended like many other dogs. The floor was being freshly laid and the cement and other dust must have given him the infection. We noticed blood in the urine and took him to the Vet, who advised admission and parenteral antibiotics. We felt very bad for Rover. Cindy, the Golden Retriever was alone at home and missed Rover. When we returned after admitting Rover, Cindy started sniffing our clothes. For the next two days Cindy was very excited to sniff our clothes after our visit to Rover. We realised how much Cindy was missing her companion. Rover on his part was equally excited when we visited the hospital. Apart from the joy he expressed on our visit, he would also smell Cindy on our clothes. After a couple of days, Rover was discharged and our ordeal ended.

Cindy, the Golden Retriever was very docile. When Cindy came to heat, Rover started behaving abnormally. Before we could make out the changes in Cindy, Rover was aware of it. Rover stopped eating. He would always be by the side of Cindy. When offered food, Rover would go around the container in circles but refused to eat anything. Rover hated rain and would run for cover. But, during this period with Cindy enjoying the rain, Rover would also stand still with Cindy with a wry expression. Many times, Rover would try to mount Cindy but without any success. Then, it so happened that there was a small mound of sand and Rover climbed over it when Cindy was close to the mound. That was the amount of desperation in Rover.

One of our friends had a female Pomeranian and requested whether he could take the services of Rover. The female Pomeranian delivered four puppies in due course and we were allowed to pick one for ourselves. We picked a female and brought her home at six weeks of age. We named her Sheeba. Sheeba grew up to be a beautiful Pomeranian with silky white lustrous hair and sparkling eyes. She was half the size of Rover and very cuddly. Sheeba used to sleep on our cot in the night. Sheeba was so small that it was difficult for her to jump on to the cot by herself and had to be helped each time.

Once, while taking the dogs out for a walk which included Cindy, Rover and Sheeba, we turned around to see that Sheeba was missing. The dogs were without a leash. We could hear a faint whine and realised that it must be Sheeba. We retraced our steps. There was a small pit on the footpath into which Sheeba had fallen. Any other dog of a little bigger stature would have gotten out on its own. But poor Sheeba kept whining to draw our attention. Within no time we helped her out of the 'pit' and soon Sheeba joined her companions.

Mongoose feeding

Within a year or so, Sheeba had matured and this was noticed by Rover, her father. Rover became very possessive of Sheeba and wanted to mate with her. Sheeba was not receptive at all and would growl at Rover. Rover would not eat anything just like earlier when Cindy was in heat. We were not allowed to touch Sheeba. The moment we went close to Sheeba, Rover would charge at us thinking that we would do something to her. One fact which we have observed over the years is that when animals are fondled too much and given a lot of love and affection, they do not breed. Sheeba was in a similar situation. Somehow Rover had managed to impregnate a reluctant Sheeba. In due course of two months Sheeba delivered. But, the puppies were not viable and we lost Sheeba also in the process of delivery. It was a bad sight as if one of our own family members had passed away.

Once, a couple from Australia had come to visit Bangalore. They were friendly and spent some time with us. They were fond of our dogs. We had warned them that Rover was very moody and to be careful. Sheeba was very docile and friendly. It so happened, that they carried Rover in their arms and posed for photographs. All the while, they were thinking that they were carrying Sheeba. Rover, on his part, played cool without throwing any tantrums and we were all surprised. To be on the safer side, we cautioned them, telling them that they were carrying Rover and not Sheeba.

Rover, in the heat of excitement, would get into a neurological problem. We had observed this about two or three times in a year. At the height of excitement, he would suddenly develop a limp and would be unable to run. He would drag his feet as though he was paralysed. After a few minutes, with the frenzy dying down, Rover would become normal. Nobody was able to pinpoint the problem.

During one of the frenzies, Rover had a similar problem. Unlike other times, Rover did not recover fully. Apart from that, Rover was unable to drink water or swallow food. During the late seventies, there were not many facilities available like X-ray and other investigations for dogs. I requested one of the nursing homes which had an X-ray facility to radiograph Rover's throat to see whether there was any foreign body lodged in the throat. The X-ray did not pick up any abnormality. It was then concluded that it was part of the paralysis that had affected Rover. Without being able to eat or drink, it was a foregone conclusion that it was a matter of few days of survival for Rover. We were all very sad that such an aggressive and lovely dog had to end up in this manner.

Sheeba, Rover's daughter, used to play very well with us. She would fetch a ball and also drop it into our hands to continue the game. After throwing the ball with our hands for some time, we would get tired. Instead of bending down each time to pick up the ball, one of us would kick the ball. This was not liked by Sheeba, at all. She would protest vehemently by staring at us and growling. She would continue to do so till we picked up the ball in our hands and tossed it in the correct manner. If we were to repeat kicking the ball, Sheeba would do a mock attack at our legs and made sure that we tossed the ball properly.

Cindy, our Golden Retriever, was a big dog. She too, would get on to the mattress and sleep with us. She would occupy a large space, but we would not mind. One day in December, with the weather being cold, we put a blanket on Cindy and made her sleep with us on the cot. We got up in the morning as usual. Cindy preferred to continue her snooze. After a couple of hours, the maid came to clean the house. After some time, the maid told us that she had not cleaned one of the rooms as somebody was sleeping and did not want to disturb them. We were surprised. Then, all of us realised that the maid had mistaken Cindy to be a human being, sleeping with the blanket fully covering her. We all had a good laugh.

Cindy was one of the most obedient dogs. We had seen dogs obeying their masters at dog shows. But Cindy, without any formal training, was exceptional. She would obey our commands without any problems and could understand our thoughts before we could express them. This way, Cindy was very reliable. Taking Cindy for a walk was a wonderful experience. There was no need for a leash. No running ahead or jumping up and down. Cindy was always composed. At that time, we had to go to the market a couple of times in a day. Cindy would accompany us only if she was called. She would not make a fuss at being left behind, unlike other dogs. Without a leash, she would come obediently at heel. She would not go sniffing at the bases of trees for scents of other dogs. She would not scare other people on the streets. When we had to cross a road, and we did not want Cindy to come, we would just say 'SIT', and she would be there till we got back. This behaviour did not go unnoticed by the passers-by. Many of them enquired about where they could train the dogs. It was always an enviable moment for both, Cindy and us.

Cindy was very gentle in nature. To give an example – a sparrow had come into the backyard and was unable to fly back. It lay fluttering in one corner. After some hectic efforts, it lay still. Renewing its energy after a period of rest, it started fluttering again. Cindy heard the commotion and went to the backyard. We were not aware of what was happening. Cindy picked up the helpless sparrow in her mouth. We thought that it was too late to save the sparrow since one bite of Cindy's would crush the bird. To our surprise, Cindy brought the bird to where we were standing, and gently dropped the sparrow into our hands. Cindy did not want to see the bird die and it was very evident by this gentle act of hers. We immediately took the sparrow and inspected to see whether there were any injuries. The wings were alright and there was no reason why the sparrow could not fly. Maybe it had become exhausted. We put a few drops of water to rejuvenate the bird. After resting for some time, we took the bird to the terrace and set it free. The sparrow flew without any effort and disappeared from our view. We thanked Cindy profusely for the kind act. Cindy knew that she was being appreciated and reciprocated by vigorously wagging her tail.

During the same period as Cindy and Rover, we got three Cocker Spaniels – two black and one fawn. The two blacks were females – Lulu and Blacky – while the male was Max. They were six weeks old. Initially, we had all the dogs inside the house for most of the time. When they became a little older, we would leave them on the terrace for most of the time, where they would play. We would go up and play with them, and also bring them down to take them for a walk. The problem was that all three dogs would relieve themselves on the terrace. This became a habit. We would clean the terrace once in two days. Most of the poop would have dried with the sun beating down on them. With the dogs eating Ragi porridge and dough or rice with milk, it was quite a mound of excreta that had to be swept and disposed of.

One day, all three dogs were left on the ground floor. We had to go out for an hour or so, and thought that there would be no harm in leaving the dogs in the living area. We would keep an empty vessel at the window of the kitchen, where the milkman would pour the milk and cover it with a steel plate in our absence. Since the kitchen door was closed, we thought that the dogs could not have access to milk.

On our return, the dogs were excited as usual, and falling head over heels to draw our attention. They were barking in joy and jumping up and down. They would lick our faces when we bent down to caress them. We observed that the kitchen door was ajar and the vessel for milk was nearly empty. We, at once, knew that the dogs were up to their tricks. We were not sure which among the three the culprit was. We then saw that there were yellow stains all along the floor which we had not observed initially. One of the dogs had finished almost all the milk and also had severe loose motions. It was very easy to make out which among them had done this. I just shouted, 'WHAT IS THIS?' The guilty dog immediately slunk away with the tail between his hind legs. The innocent ones continued to play along as though nothing was wrong. Blacky was the culprit. She went to one corner and started sulking and making remorseful sounds. After a couple of minutes, I went to her. Blacky turned on to her back in abject surrender. I felt sorry for her and told her that it was okay. She could sense that I was no longer angry with her. She righted herself and licked my face to say that everything was like before, and joined the rest of her gang to continue in their mischievous deeds.

Max, the cocker-spaniel, was fond of sitting on the parapet wall in the corner of the terrace. We had to lift him physically and put him on the wall. We were a little scared that Max may fall off the parapet in a frenzy of excitement. After a couple of times, staying on the parapet became a habit for Max and we were also not too bothered about Max keeping balance. During one such period, we had left Max on the terrace and had come down for some work. After some time, we saw Max come through the gate in the ground floor and join us. The rest of the dogs were still on the terrace. Then, we realised that Max must have fallen off the parapet, a height of more than ten feet and landed in the bushes below without a scratch. He just rushed through the gate as though nothing had happened. It was a miracle that Max had not broken any bones.

Once, we went to BNP along with the three Cocker Spaniels. Since we could not take the dogs inside the park, we left the dogs in the car and proceeded to the park. After an hour, when we returned, we had a shock. All the three dogs were panting heavily. We had forgotten to lower the window to allow fresh air. Also, the sun had come up and was shining on the vehicle causing lot of heat. We were not a moment too soon in opening the car windows and giving them fresh air. All the dogs were very thirsty. Maybe, another ten minutes delay, and we would have lost all the dogs. We felt very bad for our lack of presence of mind.

Max once tested our endurance in running a 200 metres dash. It so happened that the leash on Max's collar came off. By the time my brother and I realised it, Max was moving at a distance, sniffing the bushes. We were apprehensive that once Max realised the situation he would evade us and start running. We immediately called out to Max to come to us. This was our undoing. Max appeared to be deaf and ignored our commands. When we started approaching Max he decided to run. For Bangaloreans familiar with KR Road of mid-seventies, it was a dash of more than half a kilometre. He started running from 20th Cross, KR Road, towards Tata Silk Farm. The road was not through till TS Farm and there was a block near MM industrial estate and construction of the road was in progress. Our Max ran through the obstructions till he met with a dead end and was cornered. Imagine our plight! We had run behind Max for such a length. We were totally out of breath. For Max, it was a game, for he showed no sign of exhaustion. Then, we had to carry Max back home because there was no leash. It took a couple of days for us to recover from the pain in our legs.

DOG TICKS

Dogs, as everyone knows, have ticks on their body. We had to educate ourselves about the ticks and how to get rid of them. There were not many books or internet in those days to gleam information. Initially, we thought that there were two types of ticks. One was small dark brown colored and the other was quite big and green in color. It was much later, that we realised that the dark colored was male and the bigger green one was a female carrying eggs. We would routinely run our fingers over the dog and identify the ticks by feeling them. Then, we would pluck them forcibly from their hold on the dog. These ticks are able to survive in water. They keep floating on the water for days on end and do not die. A small bottle of kerosene was kept handy and we would put the plucked ticks in them. All the ticks would die in kerosene. The tick powders were not of much use and we stopped using them.

Another interesting thing was that the ticks would get out of the body of the dogs sometimes, and climb on the walls and get into small crevices in the furniture and the wall. Once, when I was tapping my fingers on one of the wooden chairs, I saw some movement in the crevice of the wood. I could make out the small antenna of the dark male tick protruding from it. I got a small pincer and pulled out the tick and put it into the kerosene bottle. We later realised that there were plenty of those male ticks hiding in almost all the furniture and the crevices of the wall. All that was needed was a small tap near the hole or crevice and out would come the antenna. Then, the pincers and kerosene did the job. We realised that the ticks were sensitive to the vibration of the tapping and would come out to investigate. This was their undoing and they all landed at the bottom of the kerosene bottle.

TAPEWORMS

We have all heard of the saying 'Operation successful, patient dead.' Well, something similar happened to our Cocker Spaniels. Over the years, we realised that the Cocker Spaniels were eating more, but losing weight and were not that active. At the same time, we also observed that the dogs were passing worms in their motion. It did not require an expert to identify that they were tapeworms. The worms would be passed as a long tape of about four or five inches, containing many segments. This was a serious matter. We approached the Vet, who suggested the use of betel nut instead of medication. He asked us to take one round betel nut and break it into four pieces and feed the dogs with it along with their regular food. Imagine our surprise two days later! Each dog had passed at least a thousand of those tapeworm segments. We could see a small white mound with hardly any faecal matter. There were three mounds formed by the three dogs. We were very happy that the dogs had responded so well to the treatment. Our luck ran out in a couple of days. All the dogs became very weak over the next few days, and were unable to eat much. Maybe the intestines had suffered severe damage following the discharge of so many tapeworms in one go. Maybe they had suffered minute perforations in the intestine from where the mouths of the worms were yanked out following the betel nut. We could not do anything. Even the Vet had no answer. We felt very bad as we had seen all the three grow up together and give us such a wonderful time. There was a big void left by the three spaniels. The whole house was enveloped in sadness.

This incident and the deaths of Rover and Sheeba earlier, made us realise that dogs with their short life spans, would definitely die during our lifetime. This made us resolve not to have any dogs in the future and suffer mental agony at their death.

Even though it was decided not to bring any dog into the house on a permanent basis, things did not go as we wished.

It was the turn of a Black Labrador. There is an interesting story behind the entry of the Labrador. This was a well-built dog. He was not aggressive but his behaviour was very crude. The owner who stayed in 5th block, Jayanagar, had gotten it from another person in Malleswaram who was the original owner.

This Black Labrador, whom we named Blacky, was brought to our house by the second owner in Jayanagar. The problem he faced was that the dog would jump up from behind and put his forelegs on the shoulders which made him lose balance and fall. This would happen at the auspicious time when he would be doing Surya Namaskara in the morning hours. The sacred objects and water would fall to the ground and the whole exercise would be a waste. This was happening repeatedly in spite of warning the dog not to do so. This person was very religious and did not want any such unruly intrusions and profanities.

We felt sorry for the dog and said that we would take care of him. Being greatly relieved of the Labrador, he left him then and there in our house. We tried to give all the comfort and freedom in our house. One thing was certain. He did not obey any commands and was very unruly. We made him stay in the compound most of the time and allowed him inside only when we were free to take care of the havoc he would create. We were somehow able to manage his rough behaviour. He was not aggressive but was not trained to obey. After a week, one of our family friends visited us and showed a keen interest to have the dog in his place near Lalbagh West gate. After we had briefed him about the behaviour of the dog, our friend took him to his house. Blacky would be chained during day hours and in the night once the gate was locked he would be free to roam about in the compound and tackle any intruders. This went on for about a couple of days. Then, on the third day or so we got a call from our friend saying that Blacky was missing. We were a little apprehensive because dog thieves could have taken him away. But Blacky was not a dog that could be easily subdued or cajoled into eating something from the hands of a stranger. Most probably he had jumped over the compound wall and made off on his own. But where would we search for him? We just let matters lie. Three days later, the second owner from Jayanagar called up to ask about Blacky. When we told him the details, he was surprised. He told us that the original owner from Malleswaram had called him to say that Blacky had reached his home the previous day, and wanted to know what had happened. It was then that we realised the attachment a dog has towards the original owner. Blacky had not been happy with the second owner, and also with us, or our friend. The moment he had an opportunity, he made his way to the original master.

Whenever we get calls from people who want to give away their pet dog, we try to convince them not to part with the pet. The attachment a pet dog had for its master cannot be measured or seen. Only in the most extreme cases when it is impossible to keep the pet, should he be given to somebody or to an animal shelter.

BONSI – THE LHASA APSO

One of our very close friends had a Lhasa Apso, which was slightly cross-bred. Bonsi was her name – shortened from Bonsai. Bonsi was very small when compared to the regular breed of Lhasa Apso. This friend, who was quite young, suddenly died due to jaundice. The wife came to us with Bonsi and requested us to keep the dog. We could not refuse. Thus, Bonsi entered our lives.

Bonsi

Bonsi was really a queer looking dog and people would stare at her when taken for a walk. Her eyes were round and protruding, and her looks were stunning. Bonsi took a liking to me and was always with me. She would sleep with me at night without causing any disturbance to me, and not being disturbed, herself, too. Bonsi was the only dog in the house unlike in the earlier years when there was a group. Everyone liked her behaviour and her friendly nature.

Bonsi's protruding and attractive eyes had their own problems. Whenever Bonsi tried to scratch her face with her paws, she would accidentally scratch her eyes. This would cause a small ulcer on the cornea. There would be lot of watering and secretion in the eye. It would take a couple of weeks for it to heal and there would be a scar on the cornea. As one ulcer was healing another would start in the same eye or the other with this misjudged scratching. There was no way we could prevent it. We had never come across such a problem in our experience.

A funny incident occurred with reference to Bonsi. Bonsi was part and parcel of my life for many years, and she would sleep with me in the night as told earlier. I was not married at that time. When a proposal for marriage came to me and was in the final stages of negotiations, my brother (who was already married), told my would-be father-in-law that this would be my second marriage. Who would give their daughter in marriage to a person who is married and living with his wife? There was utter disbelief on my father-in-law's face and my future wife. What was happening? How could you entertain such a thing and have the courage to call another girl to the house and talk of marriage? My brother realised that the joke had gone too far and immediately defused the situation. He explained that what he meant was Bonsi was my first wife, and any girl getting married to me would be considered a second wife. All of us had a good laugh and the matter ended there. Even today, we recollect the incident, and my wife and in-laws have a good laugh.

TETANUS IN A DOG

So far, I have been talking about the different dogs we had. The article will be incomplete if I do not mention Moti, the friendly street dog. Moti was female, and very friendly. We were concerned with her health because she would come out with a crop of puppies every so often. Her health would suffer and we thought of getting her spayed (tubectomy or family planning). We engaged the services of a good Vet and fixed a date and time for it. The Vet assured us that it was very simple and could be done at home with a little aseptic precaution. We cleaned up a room with antiseptic and made ready with all necessities. Moti was very obedient and cooperated very well. The doctor gave an anaesthetic and Moti went to sleep. Within fifteen minutes, the surgery was over and Moti recovered very well. We asked the Vet whether any dressing was necessary. He said that it would not be of much use because being a street dog; she would run around and get rid of the bandage in no time. We agreed. Moti was doing fine for a couple of days. On the third or fourth day, we noticed that Moti was dragging her hind feet a little, and there was a change in her gait. We thought that it was due to the surgery, and did not give much importance. Over the next couple of days, we observed that Moti was unable to see clearly and was relying more on her sense of smell rather than sight. But Moti was eating normally. We called the Vet. He examined Moti and said that she had developed some renal problems, and hence, because of the pain, the gait had changed. But something told us that there was something more sinister. Being a doctor myself, I realised that Moti's body was getting very stiff and I suspected it could be tetanus. Tetanus among humans is nearly hundred percent fatal. I called up the Vet and asked whether a shot of tetanus injection was required prior to surgery and had we missed it. He reassured me that dogs generally do not get tetanus and they hardly give preventive shots of tetanus prior to surgery unlike humans where it is a must. Our worst fears came true and we could not do much to save Moti. It was a real pitiable sight to see Moti stiff as a board and unable to eat or drink. We felt miserable. Our intention of getting Moti sterilised was good. We expected Moti to live longer with our intervention but it turned out to be the other way. Many times, I feel we should leave it to nature when it comes to treatment of animals. They can take good care of themselves and only when they are suffering from a disease or injury, we should intervene. In retrospect, I can say that Moti's vision had suffered because the eyes could not be focussed because of the stiffness in the ocular muscles in the early stages of tetanus.

We have had the opportunity to treat and rehabilitate a number of animals in the last forty years. The list is very exhaustive.

LORIS

Loris is a primate. It is very small and nocturnal by nature. Even though it is closely related to the monkey, it does not jump around tree branches. It is very slow. It has big eyes for better vision in the dark. It hunts small insects for food. It is exploited by humans for the sake of its attractive eyes. The extract from the eye of the Loris is supposed to improve the vision in the blind. The Loris does not have a tail because the tail is required to counter balance

Slender Loris

an animal with jumping ability. There are two species in India: one is the Slow Loris, found in north India, and the other is the Slender Loris, found in the South. The Slender Loris was captured in huge numbers from the forest and many of them were tamed and kept with roadside street magicians as an attraction. All this has been stopped in the last few years by the government, keeping strict vigil and incorporating the Indian Forest Act.

We have rescued more than a dozen Loris, and have seen their behaviour at close quarters. Even though they are insectivores, they can be trained to eat fruits like plantain, grapes and such else while in captivity. A couple of insects in their diet will keep them healthy. When the Loris eats an insect, it closes its eyes as a precautionary measure. A struggling insect could injure its big eyes and prevent proper hunting by the Loris.

One particular Loris had developed severe corneal opacity, but was able to survive in captivity. We used to keep the enclosure door open at night. When nobody was around, the Loris would venture out. The overhanging telephone cable was very handy for the Loris to cross the road at that height and explore the area. By early morning, when we went to clean and feed the other animals, our Loris would be back home, fast asleep. This went on for many months. People who had not seen a Loris would be scared stiff at the sight of this small shadowy form, sneaking along the cables slowly. Of course, our neighbours knew that it was one of our pets and did not bother much.

CIVET CAT

These are small wild cats. They are known for the pleasant smell they produce from the glands near their anus. In fact, the civets are exploited for this reason. We had, at one, time four young civets. They were very young and required to be fed by hand. They were really cute, with black spots on their grey

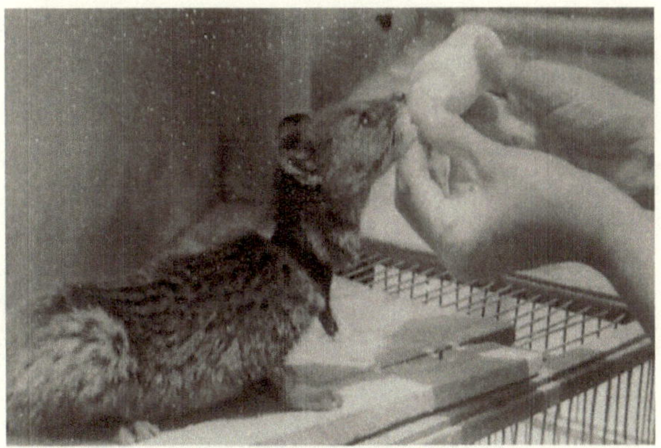
Feeding Civet cat

bodies. We prepared diluted milk, and put it in a bottle with a soft nozzle which would simulate the teat of the mother. We had to have two of them at least, because there were four of them vying for milk. We had to keep two of them in the enclosure and keep a count as to who had how many rounds of milk. By their behaviour, one could make out that one of them was very aggressive and one of them very reticent. The aggressive Civet would not stop drinking milk whereas the other required to be cajoled to fill its stomach.

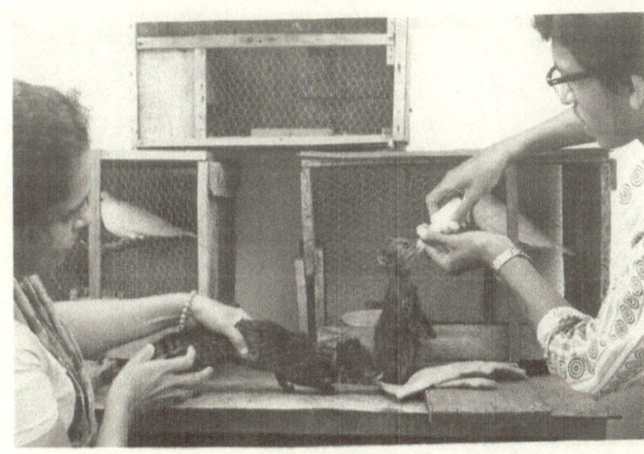
Civet cats

After a few weeks, they were ready for rehabilitation. We were already accustomed to the pleasant aroma of their perineal glands. What surprised us was that the same scent with the same intensity continued for almost two years. The Civet cats have the habit of rubbing their hind portion repeatedly against the bars of the enclosure. This is to rub their scent and mark the territory. This is done routinely in the wild. The scent is quite strong and pleasant. It is not surprising then that the civets are exploited by the perfume industry.

TODDY CAT

This cat also belongs to the Civet family but is much bigger than the Civet cat. The Toddy cat was found in the outskirts of Bangalore near plantations in the 1970s. We too have had the opportunity to house them because of habitat destruction during expansion of the city.

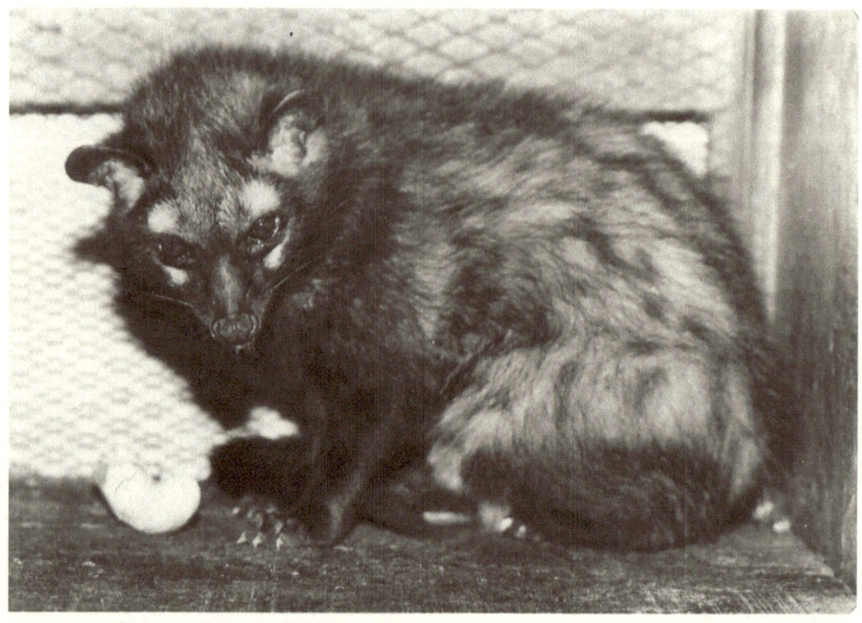

Toddy cat

ANTELOPE

TRANSLOCATION – Around the time I was finishing my anaesthesia course, our family got involved in the process of translocation of a four-horned antelope from the city (Bangalore) to BNP which is about thirty kilometres away. A gentleman, who was an animal lover, had rescued a baby four-horned antelope from the forest while driving through Bandipur reserve forest. For a few months, he faced no problem in tending to the antelope. Their house had a big compound even though it was located in the Cant area. The antelope had quite a large area to move around. Sometimes, it would enter the house and stay there, also. As the animal grew bigger, the owners started to face a new problem. The antelope started to have a liking for the curtains and bed sheets. The antelope started to chew up the clothes as though it was fodder. This became a nuisance as they could not avoid the antelope from getting into the house. Even though the antelope was tame, it would not allow people to fondle it. This way, they could not tie the animal and restrain its movement. They approached us for a solution. They wanted to shift the antelope to Bannerghatta. The officials of the Forest Department had agreed to look after the animal if they could bring it to the park. The problem was in shifting a semi-tame antelope in a vehicle for a distance of thirty kilometres without any injury to the antelope.

Being an anaesthetist, I formulated a plan of action. I had also read about what anaesthetic drugs are used for what type of animal. I knew that Ketamine would be ideal for the antelope. The dosage would probably be the same as in case of humans. The animal's rough weight was used to calculate the amount of Ketamine to be given. The drug would have to be given intramuscularly. There was no tranquiliser gun available. To give the injection, we had to hold the animal still for half a minute. We had made arrangements for three to four strong men to pin down the antelope for a brief moment during which I could give the injection. On the said date everything went according to plan. The antelope was lured to come near the owner with fresh grass which was its favourite. The three burly men then restrained it for half a minute. I was ready with the injection, and was able to give it without any spillage at the desired location. I ordered the men to stand away. The antelope made a bolt for freedom. I knew that it was a matter of couple of minutes before the drug would take over. Sure enough, the antelope started swaying and we were ready to hold it before it could collapse and hurt itself. With the help of the three assistants, we put the animal in the back seat of the car. I managed to squeeze myself in the back seat to monitor the heart and breathing of the antelope. We hoped that the effect of the drug would last for an hour by which time we hoped to reach our destination. During the journey, I would be constantly monitoring the heart with my bare hands and also the stethoscope.

On reaching BNP, without any untoward event we lifted the antelope and placed him gently on the grass inside the herbivore safari. The department officials were waiting for us. I cautioned them and the others that the animal could come out of anaesthesia at any moment. Our timing and the dosage had worked perfectly. Within a couple of minutes the antelope stirred out of its sleep. It made a couple of attempts to stand on its legs. We were ready for any eventuality. But nothing untoward happened. The antelope just shook itself out of deep slumber and started walking slowly in its new environment. There was nothing to be done from our side. The officials said that their people would keep a watch on the movement of the antelope for a couple of days through their watchers and keep us informed. There were other spotted deer and herbivores in the safari and they would make friends with the new entrant. There was no looking back, and the story ended on a happy note.

MONGOOSE

Mongoose is a very small mammal. Looks are deceptive, if one were to go by the aggressiveness of this small creature. Most of us have heard stories of how a mongoose is adept at killing snakes, particularly a cobra. It is true that a mongoose cannot only defend itself against a cobra, but is also capable of killing it. These are, Of course, manmade encounters by the snake charmers, to attract a crowd and make money. In nature, the cobra and mongoose do not fight in this manner. The mongoose is very agile when compared to a cold-blooded cobra. Energy levels are low in reptiles and they cannot sustain a fight for long. The mongoose has hairs which stand on end when excited as during a fight. The cobra tries to bite the mongoose, but cannot because its fangs will graze the hairs and not the skin. Thus, the mongoose with its agility is able to inflict effective bites on the snake without getting bitten. Nowadays, such stage-managed fights cannot be witnessed because there are strict regulations which prevent such cruelty to animals. The mongoose can defend itself against much bigger animals like the dog and scare them away.

We have had many of these graceful, friendly creatures over the years. Sometimes, we have had a pair of them together, and other times, single. If the mongoose were to be the only animal in the house, one could leave it free to roam around like a dog. Generally, they make a place for themselves in the house and seldom run away. They are comfortable in the cupboard among the clothes etc. The only problem is that when there is another animal in the house, it is better to keep the mongoose in an enclosure.

In our menagerie, the mongoose would be in an enclosure. We would go and interact with it as and when time permitted. We would put our hand inside and take it out of the enclosure and fondle it. It would jump around and play with great energy. Sometimes it would give a mock bite and run away. During feeding time, we had to be careful as most of the animals including the mongoose would be irritable. But for this, almost all the specimens have had the same temperament.

Shashidhar with Mongoose

PIGGY – THE WILD BOAR

Two young piglets were brought by some villagers one night. Looking at them, we could infer that they were young wild boars and not domestic piglets. The unmistakable whitish stripes across their grey bodies told us that they were young. The shape of their head was unlike that of a domestic pig. There were already small protuberances on either side where the future tusks were going to grow. This gave a distinct shape to the face. One of the piglets was not eating enough when compared to its sibling. We knew that it was a matter of time before it would succumb. We named the survivor Piggy. She had a free run in the house. Pigs as such love to wallow in wet mud and muddy water. Piggy was no exception. She would dig up the wet mud in the indoor garden. Her front paws and face would be fully covered with mud. With this countenance, she would jump on to the cushions on the furniture and frolic around. This would entail washing all the linen. With great effort, we could remove the mud stains which would be very stubborn against the latest detergents available in the market. This went on for a few weeks, by which time, Piggy grew by leaps and bounds. Piggy was very fond of salt biscuits and there would be a constant supply of them in the house at all times. Piggy would make guttural sounds typical of their ilk to show both irritability and satisfaction. She allowed us to touch and caress her without harming us in any way. Piggy would respond to her name and would come to us on calling, like a dog.

Looking at the way Piggy was growing, we knew that it was a matter of time before she would outgrow the domestic pig in size. We started making plans to rehabilitate her in BNP. We contacted the officials concerned and they sent us a big metal enclosure which we could use to transport Piggy. Getting Piggy inside the cage was no big deal and the journey to the park was uneventful. There was a huge fenced area in front of the leopard enclosure which had been made ready for Piggy. Piggy had a collar and leash which we used to lead her to the enclosure. We instructed the keeper with regard to Piggy's requirements. What she ate, and at what time, was very important. This way, her routine would be least disturbed. After spending a couple of hours with Piggy and giving due instructions to the keeper, we bid good bye to Piggy. We were all depressed, but it was for the good of Piggy in the long run.

Piggy, the wildboar

Two days later, there was a phone call from Bannerghatta Park. It was the keeper calling to say that Piggy was not eating anything. We were distressed and made arrangements to visit Piggy immediately. We packed her favourite foods and left. We drove our car inside the park to where Piggy's enclosure was. Piggy was not visible. The moment we honked, Piggy came bounding to the fence and started grunting loudly to show her pleasure. We wasted no time in entering the area. Piggy jumped up at us to show her affection. We did not mind the dirt coming on to our clothes from Piggy's antics. We were overjoyed to see Piggy and made her eat her choicest foods. But this was not the end of the problem. How do we manage to go so frequently for this purpose? We had to wean Piggy from this habit. We tried doing the same. But a week later, there was another semi-emergency call. Piggy had sprained her leg and was limping. We again rushed to see her. Of course, it was a bad sprain and needed restraint of movement for it to heal. We arranged for Piggy to be transported back to our place. A week of homely care and restricted movement did wonders for Piggy. It was time again for Piggy to return to her Bannerghatta enclosure. This time also, the transportation was uneventful and Piggy seemed to be happy to get back to her spacious house. We, of course, visited Piggy now and then and slowly made the visits less frequent.

It is another story of how we met Sheeba the lioness during one of our visits to Piggy. Sheeba was our guest for a year and the tales of Sheeba constitute another chapter.

SPOTTED DEER

This deer is very popular and can be spotted in National Parks like Bandipur. They stay close to human habitation because their predators do not venture out of the core areas to hunt. This way the spotted deer play safe. Even in the cities, one can see these animals in children's park where children throng to feed the deer through the fencing of the enclosure. We had the opportunity to tend to one of them. This spotted deer was brought to us from one of the nearby villages of Bangalore. It was used to human presence and had a collar on its neck by which it could be secured with a leash.

The spotted deer was transported to our place in a vehicle and arrived by afternoon. We were very eager to interact with the deer as we had not had the opportunity so far. The deer took to the new place without any fuss and we had made a place for it in the compound near the main gate. We also had fresh leafy vegetables and other goodies for the deer. The next few days were uneventful. The problem started after about a week. In the afternoon, after we had finished our lunch we went out to interact with the deer. As we were approaching the deer, we saw it go into a spasm. The whole body contorted into a vague extended shape. The deer lost balance and fell to the ground. It was no mistaking that it was a form of epilepsy or seizure affecting the whole body. Just as in humans, the deer had lost consciousness and was breathing deeply. There was froth at the mouth. The deer had a

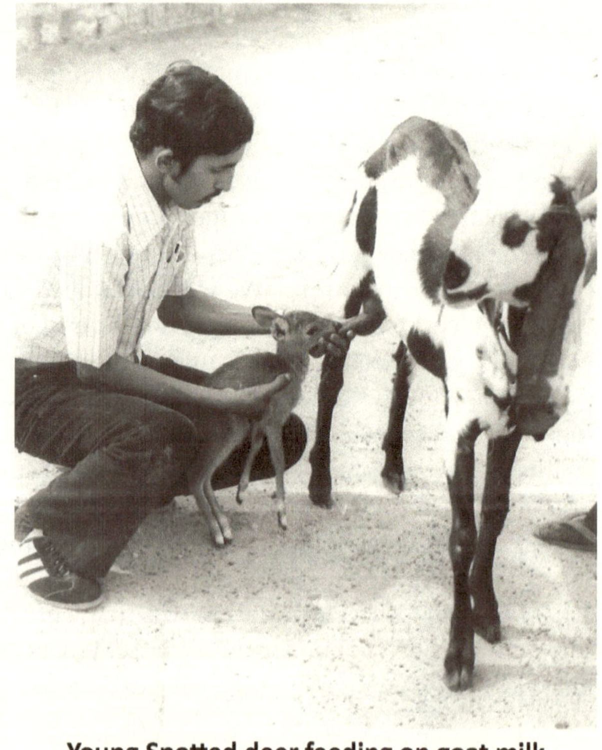

Young Spotted deer feeding on goat milk

vacant stare as the eyes were open. The whole episode must have taken a few minutes.

This was the reason why such a beautiful, friendly animal was brought to us. The original owners had not revealed any of this, suspecting that we may not accept a sick animal. Anyway, we made sure that the proper medicines were available. The drug most commonly used and available was Diazepam – a sedative which controls the seizures. We had half a dozen injections at home for emergency. The next time the deer had this spasm, we were ready to locate a vein in the deer and push the medicine into the blood stream. This way we could abort the full blown attack of epilepsy. The deer would be in a stupor for a while and then slowly get up and go about its chores. We felt sorry for such a graceful animal. We then made arrangements with the BNP authorities to translocate the animal so that the deer could be under constant supervision of a Vet.

WILD BEAR CAPTURE

This happened at a village by name Rautanahalli, near Tumkur. We got a call from some villagers by afternoon saying that a Sloth Bear was spotted in the village vicinity. The villagers had somehow managed to lure the huge Sloth Bear into a community hall of the village. Once the bear had gone inside the big hall, people had locked the door. They had to find a method to rehabilitate the bear. Someone in the village had heard about our work towards the rehabilitation of animals and put a call through. We could only give our expertise in such situations. We required trained personnel and a huge enclosure with a trap door arrangement to execute the job. Who, but the Forest 012 Department could fulfil such requirements immediately? We called up the Forest Department and apprised them of the situation and the requirements. Fortunately, they had at their disposal a huge enclosure with an upward lifting trap door. They were good enough to send a couple of their staff also. We wasted no time in driving down to Rautanahalli. It was already evening and would get dark in a couple of hours. The village had no electricity and to execute the job in darkness, would be difficult and dangerous. We had to hurry up. We had to first formulate a plan to make the Sloth Bear get into the enclosure. We hit upon the idea of placing the cage against the door of the community hall. The plan was to somehow frighten the bear from the windows on the other side, and make it rush towards the open door. The moment the bear rushed into the cage, one of us sitting on top of the cage would let the trap door fall in place. Then, the rest of the procedure would be easy. So, the cage was first put up against the closed door of the hall with great effort. The villagers also helped us in this. The village headman was told to control the crowd and keep them at a safe distance so that if at all the bear was to break loose there would not be any casualty. After placing the cage in the required position, we had to drive the bear towards the door from the other side. How would we go about it? Any amount of shouting and noise would not make the bear budge. The only thing that all wild animals fear is FIRE! We requested the villagers to provide us with half a dozen oil torches. The people had them handy because in the night they were routinely using them inside their houses and also while venturing out as there was no electricity in the village. These torches were at the end of long wooden poles of at least six feet length. We provided these torches to the village volunteers. They were supposed to put these flames through the four windows on the other side of the building and scare the bear. To further direct the bear towards the exit door, two more torches on the same side windows were thrust in. Initially, the bear got very angry. Anyone who has seen a bear's behaviour would know the force with which a bear grunts. There will be tremendous amount of air coming out of the mouth and nostril. The gush of air was sufficient to put out one of the oil torches. The bear scenting success did the same with another torch. We were left with only four burning torches. I was sitting on the cage waiting for the bear to come out of the open door and fall into our trap. Seeing two torches being extinguished brought down my spirit and also made me a little apprehensive about the outcome of this operation. As I was thinking of what to do next, things happened very fast. It was already dark and visibility was poor. There was a huge amount of noise by the watching villagers and also from the volunteers. Each of them were giving commands and expecting results. In this confusion, I saw a huge vague black form rush underneath me. Somebody shouted to drop the door, and I intuitively dropped the huge trap door. It fell with a clang. Nobody realised that the rescue operation was over. It took some time for us all to realise that the bear had rushed into the cage and was safely entrapped. We made sure that the Sloth Bear was really inside, with the help of the torch light. Everyone heaved a sigh of relief. It was the turn of the villagers to come in a line to see the vague outline of the Sloth Bear inside the cage. After their satisfaction was met, we had to lift the heavy enclosure with the animal inside, on to the vehicle to transport it. Where do we take the bear? There was a lot of discussion. Ultimately, it was decided that the bear would go the Mysore Zoo. The authorities there were informed about the arrival of the new inmate at an unearthly hour and to welcome the bear with all the necessary things.

My brother, Srinath, accompanied the bear to Mysore. By the time they arrived at the Mysore Zoo, it was past midnight. They waited till morning to release the bear in a big enclosure. It was then that they saw the Sloth Bear in the daylight. They realised that it was bigger than anticipated and it was a male. After completing all the formalities, the department staff and my brother returned to Bangalore by noon. It was one hell of an experience which to this day I remember very vividly.

SLOTH BEAR

We have all seen Sloth bears being made to obey commands on the road side. These people go around houses with a trained Sloth Bear and make them perform tricks like dancing to a beat, folding their hands etc. This is a method of livelihood for the master. Of course, one cannot see such bears now because of the strict laws of the government. The bears in such instances would have a thick rope passing through their nostrils and held at the other end by the master. One tug on the rope would make the bear cringe with pain. Their claws would also be removed to render them harmless. These things amount to cruelty to the animal. The bear is brought to submission, not out of love but through threats.

In 1976, the Forest Department brought to us a very young Sloth Bear cub. The cub was an orphan and we were supposed to tend to the bear cub. We were more than eager to have the bear cub with us. We named him Teddy. As any youngster, Teddy wanted to explore the surroundings. He made a dash to all places in the house. He even climbed the stairs and entered the rooms. After the initial excitement, he slowed down. He was careful enough as to not fall through the railings of the balcony. We decided to put a collar on him and control him with a leash just like a dog. We decided to tie Teddy to one of the pillars on the balcony overlooking the living room.

We were not sure whether Teddy was able to drink milk from a vessel. We arranged for a milk bottle with a thick nipple. Teddy finished the milk in no time. After a couple of days, we decided that only milk was in no way sufficient for the growing cub. We decided to give Ragi broth in a big vessel. Teddy did not know how to go about it. He circled this way and that, around the vessel. At last, he decided to get his front paws into the vessel and put his mouth to the broth. After a couple of futile attempts, he was able to master the technique. He made loud whistling and chortling noises to suck the broth. There was a continuous droning sound till the last of the broth was sucked in. Teddy must have realised his triumph and also relished the broth. This made him go crazy. He kept jumping up and down till he got tired. The sign of contentment in the bear is when he covers his mouth and nose with his front paws and goes into a slumber sitting on his haunches. The droning would continue unabated, rising to a crescendo and again falling to the base. This up-and-down cycle would continue for quite some time. The volume would come down to a minimum when Teddy was actually asleep.

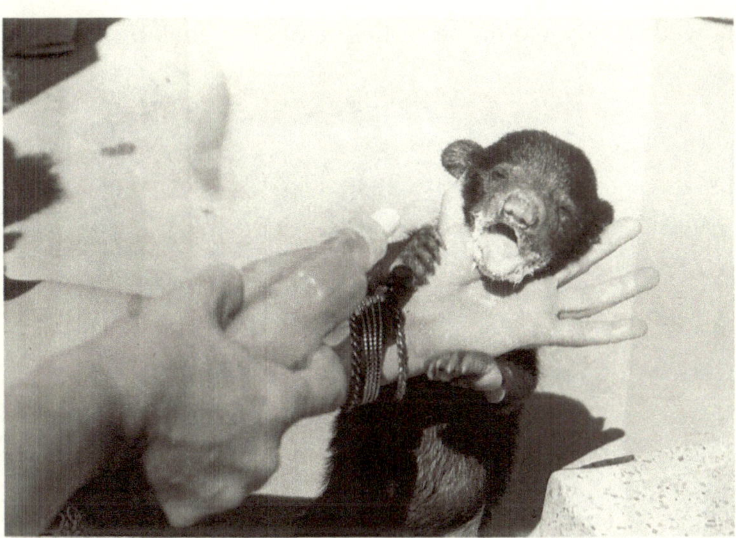

Feeding Teddy - the Sloth bear cub

Teddy in a playful mood

We made it a point to take Teddy out for a walk, every now and then. This training should be given to an animal in its formative years. Otherwise, it would become stubborn to learn anything new. Teddy was a real head turner. Who would have seen a Sloth Bear on the streets of the city going for a walk with a leash like a dog? Teddy grew into an adult and was very much attached to my mother. Before going to bed, my mother made it a point to speak to Teddy and comfort him. If this procedure was not followed, Teddy would be restless and keep making loud sounds to alert us.

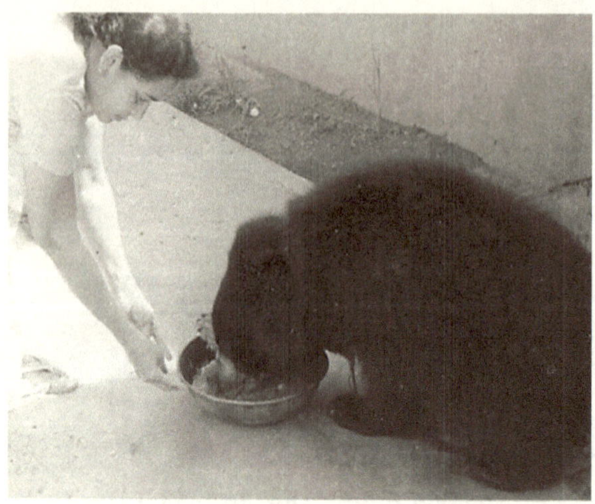

Teddy as adult

One day, my mother had to go out of station. We had not anticipated the fuss created by Teddy that night. We realised Teddy's insecurity only at night when he started vocalizing it. In addition, he showed his displeasure by hitting the big metal food bowl on the ground repeatedly. Ultimately, he threw the vessel from the first floor making us all rush out of our room. We realised that Teddy wanted to hear the soothing words of my mother. We were in a fix. Then, one of us had an idea. How about putting some old cloth of our mother near Teddy so that it could comfort him? We got our mother's dress and spread it near Teddy. He started sniffing at it. The ruckus stopped. Teddy slowly settled down. After some time, we saw that Teddy was happily sleeping on the cloth making gurgling noises of contentment.

After a couple of years, one day, when things were going smoothly for Teddy, we observed that Teddy was not his usual self. Something was bothering him. Consultation with a Veterinary doctor did not solve the problem. His appetite was low and any amount of cajoling did not yield any result. Slowly, his health deteriorated. We discovered at this late hour that Teddy had a huge abscess in his buttocks. The poor animal was having severe infection which had spread to his blood – septicaemia. It was too late to save Teddy. During those days, the choice of antibiotics was limited and their efficacy was poor when compared to this day. Poor Teddy succumbed to the infection.

PANGOLIN

This is a strange looking mammal. It has a narrow elongated head ending in a circular mouth. The whole body is covered with plates. One of the criteria for a mammal is the presence of hair. At first glance, it is difficult to spot the hairs which are distributed sparsely. On closer examination, the hairs can be seen between the plates. The pangolin is a type of ant-eater. It has a long sticky tongue to pick up ants and termites which is the staple diet. It is rarely seen in the forests as it is very shy by nature. In spite of this, we have had about six pangolins brought to our centre. Usually, villagers at the edge of the forest come across these pangolins. They do not and cannot bite. They are harmless. The only weapon which it uses is its front legs which are equipped with strong claws for digging purpose. They are able to dig into the termite nests and feed upon them. They have a soft unprotected belly.

Pangolins in captivity do not survive for long because of the inadequacy in their diet. It is just not possible to provide so many ants and termites every day. On all occasions except one, we had to rehabilitate the pangolin back in their jungle habitat. But, during the couple of days it was with us, we observed that they are harmless and timid. When left free in the house, they crawl into some inaccessible corner. Once, a pangolin made itself secure by hiding below a steel cupboard. One of us in the room who did not know the presence of the pangolin was surprised when the huge cupboard started swaying and made creaking noises. Every one rushed into the room to see how a huge cupboard could sway side to side. Some of us thought of the possibility of an earthquake. When we put torchlight below the cupboard, we realised that the pangolin was hiding there. Imagine the strength of this small fellow. He was able to lift the huge weight.

The pangolin refused to eat anything including small insects, cockroaches, eggs etc. We had to rehabilitate him in a hurry. The only exception to this was one pangolin which somehow had a liking to milk and eggs. The beaten egg mixed with milk was lapped up within no time, leaving us all surprised. This was really surprising. No such literature was available regarding pangolin's diet in captivity. We were able to study this pangolin for a little longer than the others as there was no hurry to rehabilitate it. But, since the diet was not the same as in the wild, we suspected that over a period of time it could become weak. Hence, arrangements were made to rehabilitate the pangolin in the Herbivore Safari at BNP.

SQUIRREL

The common three-striped squirrel has been a regular inmate of the rehabilitation centre. Squirrels of different age groups starting from those pink colored, no hair and eyes not opened, to adults with injuries have been brought to us for nursing. Of course, very young ones do not generally survive with the best of nursing care. The problem is that the composition of milk is not the same as that of the mother. After feeding the young ones, almost all the mothers, be it of the squirrel or a lion, lick the abdomen of the young ones forcefully. This is very important for the young ones to digest the food. Such minute things are often not noticed by the humans and the young ones succumb for the lack of such care. As per our experience, only those squirrels with a little hair and open eyes survive to become adults. That is the level of maturity needed. Warmth is most essential, particularly in winter months. Many squirrels have been given to us along with the nest. This makes things better for the squirrel to survive.

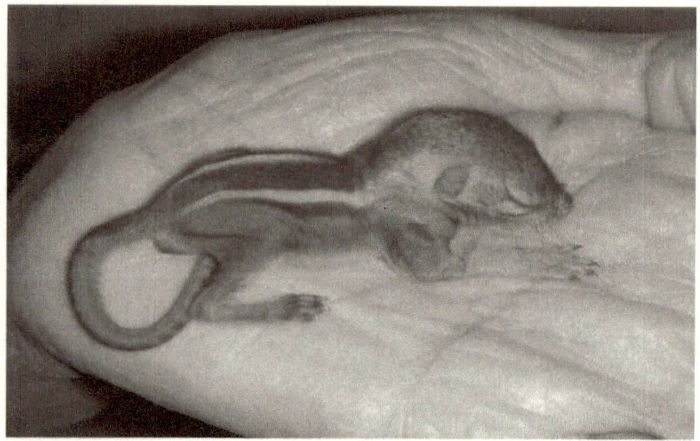

Young Squirrel

The negative side of this rehabilitation process for most of the animals is that the young ones take it for granted that food will be available for the asking. They do not have any hunting skills to procure the food on their own. There is no mother to guide them in the ways of life. They do not know that predators are waiting to pounce on them, the moment they step

Adult Squirrel

out of the cage. They have never been exposed to such dangers. These factors make it difficult to rehabilitate the animal back in the wild. They become misfits. For this reason, many animals including the squirrels have to be kept in spacious enclosures and cannot be returned to the wild.

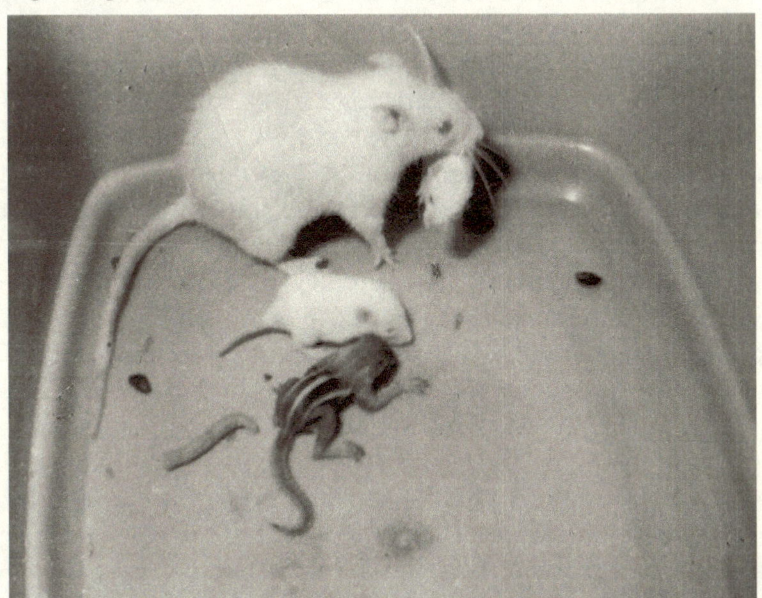

Trying to make the lactating mother mouse feed the young squirrel

Being kept in enclosures without good exercise and plenty of food has its own problem. They develop obesity just like human beings. Not only the caged animals, but even dogs are overfed with little exercise. Many dogs being taken for walks can be seen to be on the plumper side. Our rescued squirrels were no exception. Many of them could not jump and be agile like their brethren in the wild. But, many of these animals outlive their kind in the wild because of good food and protection from predators. In fact, it has been documented that animals in captivity live longer. The normal life span of a squirrel in the wild has been estimated to be around four or five years. We have documented proof of one squirrel which lived to the ripe old age of eleven years! This could be a world record.

Lord Rama was supposed to have blessed the squirrel with his three fingers causing the stripes to appear. The squirrel had helped Lord Rama in a small way by bringing pebbles in its mouth to help build the bridge to Lanka.

MONKEY WITH PUPPY

It might seem very strange. What a combination! Well, one day, out of the blue, a monkey was spotted near our residence. For some reason it preferred our house and came inside. It did not create any havoc. It was a female. There were no other monkeys accompanying her. Very surprisingly, this monkey was carrying a black colored puppy. The pup could have been a month old. How did the monkey come across this pup and what instinct made her adopt it as her young is an enigma. The monkey was very alert and possessive about the pup. No one could approach the pup without being intimidated by the monkey. What strange behaviour was this? The monkey would eat fruits and other edibles and offer the same to the pup by placing it in front of its mouth. The poor pup was totally lost without its original mother. It would keep making whining noises which would have drawn the attention of its mother. The monkey was totally unmoved by such sounds. The monkey appeared to be tame and used to humans. She did not threaten any of us except when we approached the puppy. To add to the woes of the puppy, the monkey would climb the grill of the gate and place the pup on the gate bar which was very narrow. It was a real balancing act for the pup. The monkey would repeatedly lend support to the pup so that it would not fall.

We realised that more than the monkey, the pup needed attention. The monkey was showing utmost affection towards the pup, but it was not enough. The pup was definitely hungry and needed milk at least, if not some solid food. The problem was to separate the pup from the monkey. With her protective, motherly instinct, the pup could not be separated from the monkey. We also noticed that the monkey was very sleepy but the pup was preventing the monkey from catching forty winks. We waited for an opportune moment to separate the two. After gaining the confidence of the monkey that we meant no harm, we waited for the monkey to go into a slumber. With the pup a little away from its foster mother, we quietly picked up the pup and took it to a safe distance where we had a bowl of milk ready. The puppy was ravenously hungry and within no time had emptied the bowl and asking for more. Once its hunger was satiated, we put the puppy back near the monkey.

The night was spent in this manner without any untoward incidents. Morning dawned and the same thing continued. We were wondering whether the monkey had lost her real young one recently and would this be the reason for such peculiar behaviour? But, looking at the mammary glands of the monkey it was improbable. After some time, the monkey decided to set off elsewhere with the young pup beside her. That was the last time we saw the monkey in that area.

BAT

Bats are nocturnal mammals. They are the only mammals with flying ability. There are mainly two types of bats. One is very small and eats insects like small flies and mosquitoes, which is called the Pipistrelle, and cannot be kept in captivity as it eats only insects which are difficult to procure, and eats them in flight. The other is the Fruit Bat which resembles a small rat with wings. These can be kept in captivity as they eat fruits like banana, grapes, papaya etc. Of course, it takes some time for the bat to get used to this type of diet. In this manner, a bat can survive for years. We had a Fruit Bat which was brought to us about sixteen years ago. Bats rest upside down on trees and a similar environment should be provided for them in captivity.

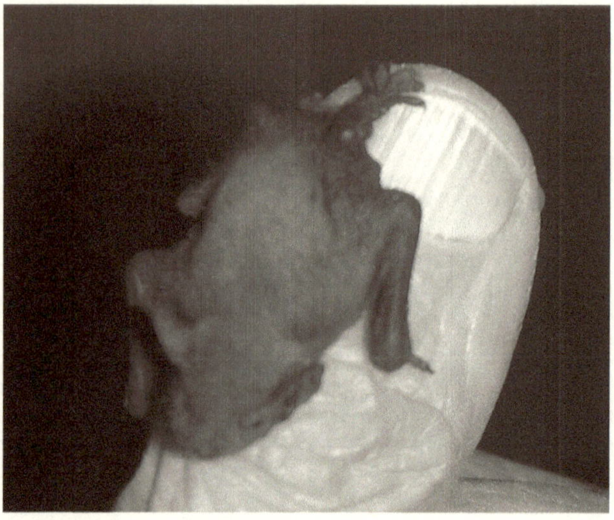

Pipistrelle

Bats rely upon echo location to search for objects or to avoid them as the case may be. The sound emitted by the bat cannot be heard by human beings. The bat keeps fluttering its ears. This is to pick up the echo of its own sound. Thereby, it locates obstacles and is able to fly around without bumping into any.

Bats are carriers of rabies and one should be careful not to get bitten by them. There are also Vampire-bats, which drink blood as their exclusive diet. Usually, cattle and pigs are the victims and humans can also be targets for the Vampire-bats.

OTTER

Otters are aquatic mammals. They are the size of a domestic cat. They have a heavy flat tail which they use as a rudder. They are great swimmers and eat fish. One of the traders at the fish market contacted us to say that they had caught an otter along with other fish and whether we could provide shelter for the otter.

Otter

Otter eating fish

The otter was quite friendly and would play with us as though he was used to humans. We put him in an enclosure and would let him out when necessary. The otter refused to eat the meat offered to other carnivores in the menagerie. The otter was used to eating only salt water fish. The problem was that most of the traders in the market would sell fresh water fish only. Salt water fish was sold only in a few areas of the city. It was a big problem to procure the delicacy every day. But, somehow it had to be done. Being vegetarians added to the problem. We were accustomed to feeding fresh raw meat to the inmates with the help of tongs and tweezers. But, feeding fish was different and difficult.

Ultimately, we found a place for him in the Mysore Zoo. Relevant arrangements were made and the Otter was provided with more natural surroundings.

BIRDS

The following birds have been rescued and rehabilitated at our centre.

OWLS

1. **THE GREAT INDIAN HORNED OWL:** This is the biggest owl in Asia. The name is because of the two horn-like structures on either side of his head. All owls have big eyes for nocturnal vision. Unlike many other birds the owls cannot move their eyeballs. Hence, they make a comical circular movement of the head to focus better on the object. This is because the eye ball is tubular and not spherical as in other birds. Owls prey on rodents. Their flight is silent because of tertiary feathers along the edge of the wings. The rodent which is eaten whole is digested and the undigested matter like the skin and hair is vomited out. This is called a pellet – owl pellet. By studying the size and composition of the pellet one can guess as to what owl it could be. The Great Horned Owl looks very fierce and makes a loud hissing noise to scare away any intruder.

2. **MOTTLED WOOD OWL:** When compared to the Great Horned Owl, this owl is very cute. It is not very fierce looking. Its face is round and it is friendly. In fact, one of the specimens used to fly on to our laps and sit around for some time as we caressed its head and neck. All birds have a third eyelid which is translucent and covers the eye while the bird is resting. It is very clearly seen in these big owls as their eyes are big and prominent. In the adjoining photograph it is seen being taken out for a walk along with the Sloth Bear.

Teddy and owl out for a walk

Young Mottled Wood Owl

Mottled Wood Owl sun bathing

Mottled Wood Owl

3.   **OWLETS:** These are small owls and there are many species. We had Spotted Owlet, Scops Owl and such else. These birds also behave similarly as their bigger counterparts. The diet for these owls would be small pieces of meat. It is always preferable to add a little roughage in the form of skin of the prey. This is to ensure that the digestive system behaves as normally as possible.

Spotted Owlets

4. **BARN OWL:** We have had at least about thirty barn owls in a span of twenty years. These owls have a typical heart shaped face. The mother would have abandoned the nest due to some disturbance and the young ones would be brought by the public or we would be informed regarding the same. Usually, there would be a set of three young ones. They would be white in color due to the down feathers. These feathers would be shed as the bird grew and would be ultimately transformed into the typical brown with spots. The barn owls have a high pitched screech. Hearing the screech of the captive birds we have had the wild ones coming and visiting their kin.

Young Barn owls

At one time, we had about five barn owls. We had constructed a flight cage for them so that they could freely flap their wings and fly from one end of the cage to another. This would ensure good exercise for them and keep them healthy. These barn owls were rescued when they were very young with the down feathers still on them. They could not be rehabilitated as they could not adapt themselves to a life in the wild. They would not know how to hunt on their own. Training such birds to hunt was out of the question as there were no facilities available. All the barn owls were quite happy and comfortable in their present environment. It so happened that they were all struck with a form of bird virus. Within two days all the birds succumbed to the virus. They just stopped eating the food provided to them in the night and were seen sitting on the floor. Any bird which is a rooster (perch on a branch) found sitting on the ground is sick. This is because they have lost the strength to maintain their balance on the perch. They require immediate attention.

We also observed over the next few days that the screeches of the wild barn owls were no longer heard and they were no longer spotted in the vicinity. This led us to believe that all birds of that species must have succumbed to the deadly virus.

MYTHS ABOUT OWLS: Many people in India believe that the owl is inauspicious. If it were to sit on the roof of any house, then that house would have a death in the family. For this reason, owls would be chased away and not allowed near any residence. Once, a visitor to our menagerie, after viewing the animals was interested to know whether we could give him an owl for a few days. We were surprised and wanted to know the reason. He came out with a peculiar reason. This person had rented his house to a tenant who was refusing to vacate the house. The tenants were very orthodox people and believed the owl to be a bad omen. Taking this opportunity, our visitor wanted to put the owl in that house and scare the tenants away so that he could take possession of the house. Anyway we refused to oblige.

BARBETS

These are green colored birds which can be heard singing their typical songs, high in the foliage of trees both in the city as well as in the parks. They are rarely seen as they merge so well with the greenery. There are many species of barbets. What we had was the green barbet. There must have been at least fifty of them over a period of twenty years. Most of them had come to us as very young ones and were used to being hand fed with bananas till they reached a stage of self-help. Without the mother teaching them what to do and when, it was very difficult for the birds or for that matter any animal to be independent as adults. These factors always come into play in the rehabilitation process of any bird or animal. Even if the enclosure is large enough for many birds of the same species, we learnt that it was better to allocate one enclosure for one bird. There is something called the PECKING ORDER among birds and BITING ORDER among animals. This is nothing but hierarchy. For example, if there are four barbets in the same enclosure there is going to be a dominant barbet which will boss over the others and there will be the least dominant barbet which would not be allowed freedom of movement and also feeding when hungry. If the observer did not notice this and left the situation to continue, then over a period of few days you could find the least dominant bird on the ground, weak with hunger and exhaustion. This is because the dominant bird will not allow the weaker one to even feed. This is the main reason for isolating each bird in its own enclosure so that there is no threat of any sort. The pecking order is decided by one bird assessing the other by sight or by challenging the opponent to a fight to decide on superiority. There is never a fight to the finish because nature does not want any animal to perish in the process of establishing the hierarchy.

The barbets were quite content in their respective enclosures. They would feed basically on bananas and also seasonal fruits like cherries, grapes etc. The perch for these were placed at a height of about two feet from the ground. The bottom of the enclosure was covered with mesh on which a sheet of paper was spread. This was to make the job of cleaning the cage easy. Every day, the paper would be replaced with a fresh one. The barbets were the only birds to face a peculiar problem. The barbet would come to the ground and walk around on the paper. In the process they would somehow get their own excreta on to their toes which would dry up. Over a period of ten to fifteen days the muck would get accumulated to such an extent on their toes that all the toes would be buried in their own excreta. The barbet would have a big ball of its own excreta at the tip of the legs and would not be able to sit on the perch. The ball would ultimately get very hard and the poor barbets would be unable to dislodge them. We had to physically catch hold of the barbet, restrain them from biting, and with the help of another person, the hard ball had to be broken with great force. It was very important that the delicate tips of the toes were not injured or yanked during the process of treatment. For this the hard mass had to be soaked in water for few minutes. Only the outer-most layer would come out after repeated scraping. The inner most nucleus would just dislodge after some time, leaving the bare toes.

COCKATIEL

These are exotic birds and not native to India. They are kept in captivity and are very friendly. The cockatiel that came to us was given to us by a family which had the bird earlier. Since they were migrating, they had to pass the bird to us for proper care. This cockatiel was very friendly and allowed us to play with it. Most of the time, we would let the bird out and allow a free run- or fly- around the house. The cockatiel would most of the time sit on our shoulders while we carried out our work. During lunch, tea and dinner one could find the bird on the dining table and trying a get a titbit. Only during the night the bird would be secured inside a cage.

PEACOCK

 Peacocks along with peahens are generally kept as pets in South Indian temples. Muruga temples usually have them as it is the vehicle for the God Muruga. Each Indian deity has his own animal as a vehicle like the Brahminy Kite is for Vishnu, the rat for Ganesha etc.

Peacock

One day, some temple workers from the nearby Muruga temple brought two Pea hens. The peahens were very poor in health and unable to stand properly. On examination, it was found that the feet of the birds were full of wounds and hence the poor birds could not stand or move about on their feet. We were wondering as to what could be the reason for both birds to have a similar problem. We wanted to see the place where the birds were kept. There was a huge quadrangle in the temple premises with a concrete floor. The birds had no access to any other place covered with mud. This was the problem. The birds with their delicate feet were accustomed to a mud floor. Like other hen of their ilk, they are used to scratching the mud to find food. This is the way any bird of the HEN family behaves. When the peahens tried to do this, their feet would constantly rub against the hard concrete and get injured. There was no way it would heal because the hens continued to be kept in the same place without any soft material. We immediately applied some antiseptic to the feet of both the birds and covered their feet with soft cotton. With good treatment and natural mud surface the peahens were on the road to recovery in a couple of weeks. We advised the temple authorities on the need to give proper environment to the birds. In a lighter vein, we also told them that Lord Muruga would be very angry and curse them for not looking after his close companion – the peafowl. They promised to provide all the facilities suggested by us.

Pea hen

PARAKEET

People often confuse the parrot and the parakeet. How does one differentiate between them? Well, there are no parrots in India. The long tailed green birds which we commonly see is the parakeet. Parrots do not have a long tail.

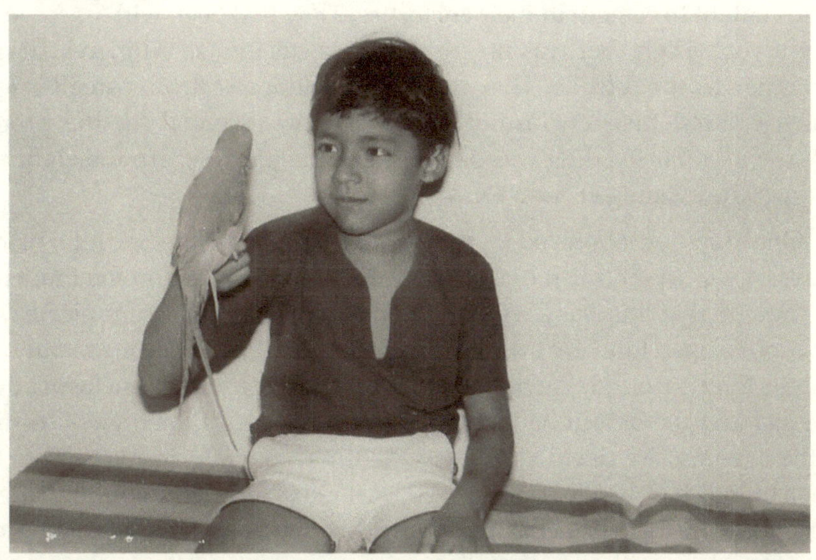

Rose-ringed Parakeet

We had the Rose-ringed Parakeet. The males have a rose ring around their neck and the female a black one. The male was very friendly and would sit on our shoulder and allow us to touch him. While having lunch or tea he would fly down to the table and ask for small bits of snacks without hesitation. He survived for about thirty years with us. He would also peep into our mouths and pick up titbits sticking between our teeth.

One of the rescued female parakeets developed a tumour in her eye and went blind in both eyes. Since her vision was hampered she would be always irritable and had to be cajoled into accepting our presence. She too survived for about twenty-five years.

BULBUL

These are small sparrow sized birds which are very common in the urban areas also. They can be heard chirping loudly in the early morning in the garden trying to build a nest and woo their partner. There are many species of bulbul. We had a pair of captive red vented bulbuls. They were quite content to remain in their enclosure. They had been with us for more than a year. Their diet was mainly bananas cut into small pieces, grapes and other seasonal fruits. They were quite adept in catching small insects which entered their enclosure. This was very essential for the protein requirement. The feeding was done once in the morning around eight and again in the evening around four.

One day, we observed a red vented bulbul in the vicinity of our house. It was flying from one tree to another and sitting on the branches. We thought that this was a wild bulbul that had come to communicate with the captive ones. Only by evening did we realise that it was one of our own bulbuls flying around. We noticed that for some reason the enclosure door was ajar and the bulbul had made good its escape. At the time of feeding in the evening, we decided to keep the door open. For some reason, the other bulbul had not flown out. We least expected the bulbul outside to come back in to the enclosure to feed on the fresh fruits. Imagine our surprise when within half-an-hour the escaped bulbul was back in its enclosure along with its companion happily eating the fruits. We wasted no time in securing the door of the cage.

PARIAH KITE

These are the predatory birds which are commonly seen flying high in the air riding the hot air current. They can also be seen near sewage lines in the city trying to grab a morsel of food from the sewage. Many of them are seen sitting along the fence bordering the sewage. They are brown in color. They have keen eyesight like other predatory birds. Sometimes, these birds get injured by accidentally hitting against an electric cable and fall down. Sometimes, they could be found sitting on the ground for a few hours due to sheer exhaustion. People have brought such birds to us for treatment. When such an exhausted bird is brought in for treatment, one should just leave the bird alone in an isolated area like the garden. A pot of water and if possible a few cut pieces of meat should be kept near the bird. One should observe the kite from a safe distance without disturbing it. Many times, it is seen that the kite takes rest for a couple of hours, has a drink after gobbling the meat pieces and just takes off in the sky as though nothing was wrong. This is due to heat exhaustion and nothing else. No other treatment or nursing care is required.

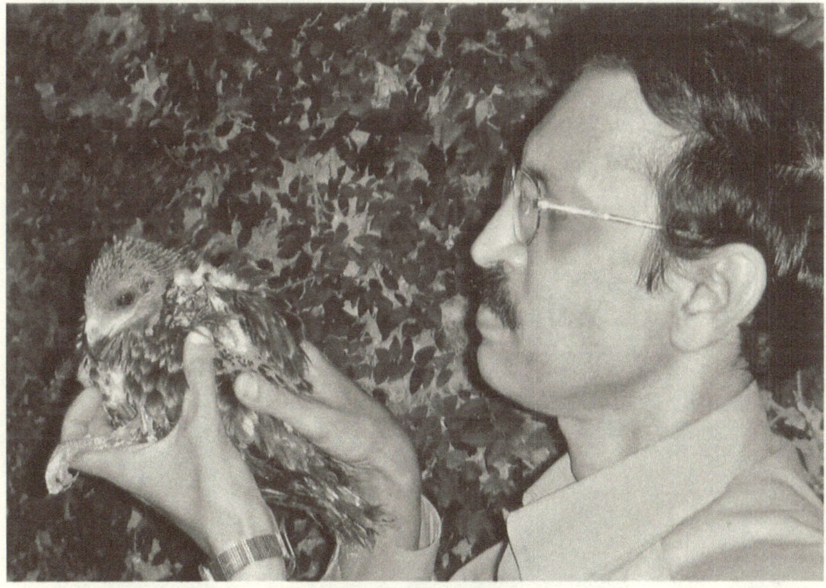

Pariah kite injured

If the kite happens to be young and stays longer with the humans, it is often seen that they are reluctant to fly back to freedom. They can be trained to sit on the forearm or the shoulder. They can be taken for a 'walk', on the streets without the least bit of fuss from the kite. One has to be careful about the talons which can dig deep into the flesh when the bird tries to balance itself on the forearm. After some practice, both the bird and the trainer get used to each other and know how to avoid injury or keep balance. Even though the beak is strong, the kites do not use it to attack. It is the talons which come into play during attack. Some kites brought to us were very badly injured in the wing making them a cripple for life. Such birds have to be taken care of till the end. One particular kite was having only one leg. There was only a stump remaining of the other. But otherwise the kite was quite healthy.

Pariah kite

For the sake of the more scientific minded readers, I would like to mention here that the eyesight of the kites and other predatory birds like the eagles, hawks etc, is very keen. Not only are they able to focus on something on the ground from high above in the sky but also able to adjust their focus as they swoop down on the prey without losing focus. This adjustment has to be done very fast. For example, you are asked to thread a needle and immediately watch TV at a distance of twenty feet. It is very difficult for humans to change focus rapidly. This is called the accommodation reflex which is very good among these birds. Another relevant piece of information is that the central focus of vision in the eye –called the fovea, are two in number, whereas humans have only one. This is the reason for acuity of vision or sharpness.

KESTREL

These are predatory birds which are little bigger than the crow. They are not as common as the pariah kite which is seen circling high in the sky. The Kestrel sometimes gets injured like the kites, as mentioned earlier. There was one instance of the Kestrel which was nursed back to health and refused to fly off. With a lot of hesitation this Kestrel finally took off. We were all very happy for it. But, this Kestrel wanted to show its gratitude and could be seen circling above in the same vicinity. At the time of feeding in the evening it could be seen hovering over the terrace. When we threw a piece of meat high up in the air, imagine our surprise when it swooped down to grab it and flew away with the morsel in its talons. This continued for several days. Once, when there was a delay in feeding the inmates, we were surprised to see the Kestrel waiting for its share in the living area upstairs. The bird had flown through the open door of the terrace and was patiently waiting for us to keep up the rendezvous. After several weeks, we lost track of the Kestrel. Maybe the time had come for it to find a mate, for it was the beginning of the mating season.

There are many lessons to be learnt from the above incident. Many people are of the opinion that birds should not be kept captive and full freedom should be given to them. This is true but there are exceptions to this. When a bird is rescued in the wild, a proper enclosure must be provided for them. It so happens that these birds which were leading their life in the wild suddenly find themselves in a captive state. Over a period of few days, the bird generally feels very comfortable in the present environment as long as the proper food, water and habitat are provided for them. They no longer crave for freedom. There is no need for them to hunt for food. There is no competition from others of their species. There is no fear of any predator. These birds which get accustomed to this easy life find it very difficult to get back into the wild and may become misfits. This is one of the reasons why the bird or animal should be rehabilitated as early as possible. The bird or animal loses its predatory or foraging skills. In fact, with such good conditions prevailing in the captive state, many of them put on excess weight and may suffer from problems of plenty, just like the humans. One thing is certain from our experience. When good care is given to these rescued birds or animals, they outlive their normal lifespan as is evident from our records. One thing to be noted is that an injured bird or animal is better off in a small enclosure because it cannot hurt itself by flapping or running around the place and exhausting itself in the process. Also, it is better to keep them in a dark place or cover the enclosure so that they do not get frightened in their new environment.

It is the opinion of many, that there should always be a companion for the inmate. Many visitors have expressed that there should be company for the solitary bird or animal. This is not true. Most of the time, there will be unnecessary fights when there is more than a single animal. This is usually to establish hierarchy as narrated before. Even when the two animals or birds are of the opposite sex, this conflict is seen. It is only when the female of the species comes to oestrus that the male is aroused and attempts are made at mating. Otherwise it is not necessary that a male and female should get along well in the limited space of the enclosure.

NIGHT HERON

Night herons are water birds like their cousins the pond heron. Night herons are dark grey in color. They feed mainly on aquatic small animals like fish and frog. These birds usually nest in tall trees. People familiar with the Basavanagudi area of Bangalore may recollect the avenue of tall trees on KR Road near National College. The cackling of the hundreds of birds nesting on these trees could be heard in the evening apart from the copious droppings dotting the footpath and the street.

The night herons would bring forth their young ones in the month of June and July every year. Unfortunately these are the months when the wind is very intense. Many young ones or the nest with the young ones would be toppled from great heights. The young ones were likely to perish. Many young night herons have been brought to our Trust after these mishaps. The young night herons would have a fracture on one or both of their legs. We have taken such night herons to the Veterinary hospital. The doctors there would put a cast on the leg for a few weeks just like the treatment for the humans with fracture. In due course, the fracture would heal and the question of rehabilitation would arise. In this manner, dozens of young night herons have been rescued.

During the windy months, we would get at least half a dozen young herons at a time in batches. The problem was to house them in separate enclosures with space being restricted. The first time we had put about 5–6 young ones together in a big enclosure without realising the consequences. Morning rounds of the menagerie had a couple of casualties. The young night herons had had a fight for pecking order. The stronger ones had repeatedly jabbed at the weaker ones with their beaks. The result was disastrous for the weaker ones. There were head injuries and a couple of them died. We felt sorry for them and also realised our ignorance in not separating them. We immediately put partitions of cardboard and segregated the birds. Even here we had to make the partition high enough so that the birds could not see each other. The moment another bird's head was seen, there would be something like a swordfight with their beaks.

This way, it was very difficult to tend to each bird. Feeding had to be done individually. Water bowls had to be kept for each of them. Access to each bird had to be looked into. Nursing a dozen young night herons in this manner was a Herculean task. The appetite of these growing birds was enormous. A morsel of food would go down their throat in a jiffy and they would crave for more as though they were starving the whole day. Added to this, some of the birds had a plaster cast on one or both legs which made their movement awkward and slow. They had to be given special attention.

With the chopping down of these trees in the last decade and the arrival of the Metro, these graceful birds are no longer seen in these areas. Old timers get nostalgic when they travel in these localities. The cackling of the birds and the wetness under ones feet with the droppings of these birds were more welcome than the concrete high rises which have replaced the greenery that once was.

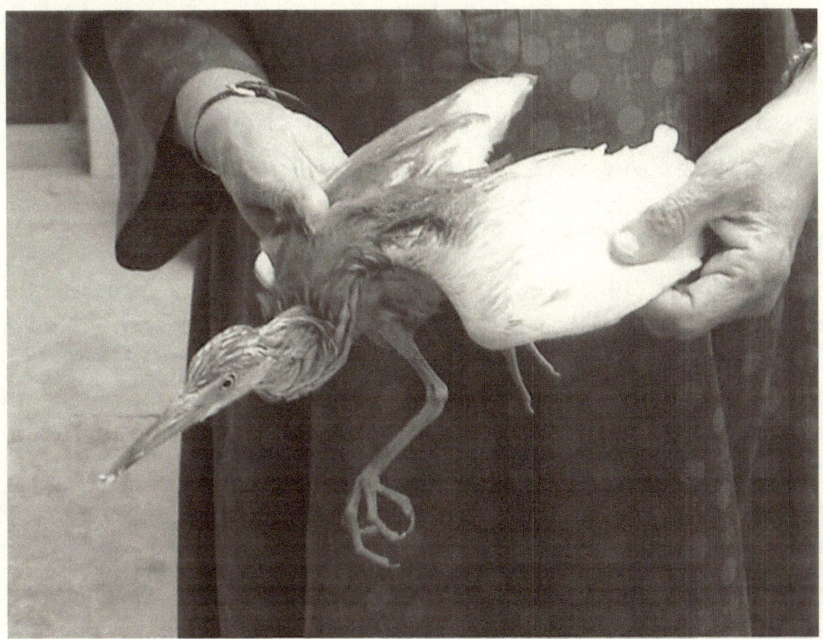

Pond heron

CROW

Even though the crow is a very common bird in all parts of India, both in rural and urban areas, it is seldom kept in captivity. One reason could be that many consider it a bad omen. Our experience tells a different story. Even though injured crows have been brought to us, they have been very few and far between. The ones which were brought to us never survived beyond a few days. Some of the crows appeared relatively healthy and young but somehow could not make it. Unlike other birds which are very choosy and specific in their diet, crows eat anything and theoretically should be able to survive. But, this has never happened. Even to this day it is an enigma and readers are most welcome to give inputs regarding this.

The White Crow, which is an aberration in nature, has been kept in captivity in some zoos. They are albinos, meaning they lack the black melanin pigment.

Even though the crow is one of the most intelligent birds, it is very surprising that the koel (Cuckoo) is able to outwit the crow by managing to lay its eggs in the crow's nest. The female crow is made to bring up the young Koels. It is a wonder of nature that the intelligent crow is not only deceived by the koel to accept its own eggs but also to bring up the young ones as its own.

Many things in nature are accepted by us without thinking twice. Has anyone thought as to how the first attempt could have been made by the koel to lay its eggs in a crow's nest? This could not have happened by trial and error. Even if it were to be so, how does the young female koel accomplish the same on attaining maturity? Surely, its mother is not there to guide it. The young koel never knows who its true mother is. Then, one has to assume that this behaviour is ingrained in the young bird from birth and surfaces during maturity. It is there in the genes. But, how did this gene form initially, if at all. Well, let us leave it at that.

KOEL/CUCKOO

The koel's behaviour has already been discussed to a certain extent in the previous lines pertaining to the crow. In contrast to the crow, Koels are very comfortable in captivity. It does not matter whether they were brought to us from a very young age or they came as adults. They subsist mainly on fruits like plantain and other berries. They become quite friendly too. The females are black in color with white spots where as the males are jet black and spotless.

A very peculiar thing that has been noticed by us over these three decades is that almost all the Koels rescued and rehabilitated by us have been females. Males would have constituted hardly about five percent. We do not know as to why only females get injured either as adults or as young ones. Even the small percentage of the male Koels have not survived in captivity.

More than half a dozen female Koels were there at a time. They would be awake at the break of dawn and would give a shrill call one after the other as though each one wanted to outperform the other. During the summer months, it was mating time for these birds. The male koel in the wild would start off with the melodious call. The females in captivity would respond by instinct. The male would again repeat its melody followed by the shrill cries of the females either in unison or in succession. This way there was no need to set the alarm clock in the morning.

Other birds which have been rehabilitated by the Trust are Purple Moor hen, Coucal, Baza, Mynah, Blue Jay, Pitta, Pigeons and doves, Darter, Hoopoe, Sparrows, Quails, Partridge, Scavenger vulture, Brahminy kite, Black winged kite, Ducks, Night Jar and African Lovebirds, among others.

Koel

Black winged kite

Brahminy Kite (Garuda)

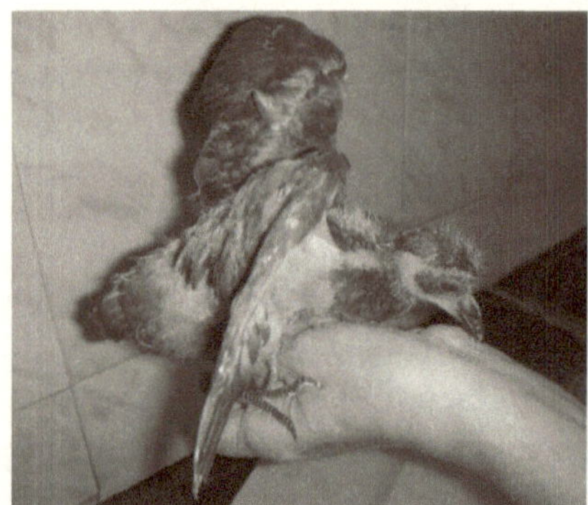

Young Dove

Ducks

Night Jar

PROPOGATION OF KNOWLEDGE regarding conservation of nature, Environmental pollution, Animal behaviour etc, apart from dispelling myths about snakes is a major agenda for the ARRT. In this regard, the Trust has organised many interactions with students of schools and colleges in Bangalore and surrounding areas. Students would come in batches to our premises. They would spend about an hour, where in, apart from seeing the different species of rescued animals at close quarters, they would be taught important facts regarding each of them.

The Trust has a large number of study materials in the form of charts, diagrams and sketches which are explained to the students. Lectures to create awareness about different snakes form the most important and interesting part of the session.

The Trust has imparted knowledge to thousands of students over the years. In fact, many of the students who had visited us in the 1980s have come back to visit us with their spouses and children. They are excited to tell their children how they had come thirty years ago to the same place and many get nostalgic.

The Trust has held many exhibitions, particularly during the Wild Life week in the first week of October for many years. The Trust has also celebrated the World Environment Day on June 5 for many years.

In 1980–1981, with the sponsorship of the Department of Environment and Ecology, Government of Karnataka, the Trust undertook a programme to educate the villagers of the various districts of Karnataka. The Trust members along with other volunteers undertook a twenty day tour of the villages in various districts to propagate the idea of conservation of nature and animals.

During this tour, we were able to unearth some facts which had not been known. One important fact that emerged was that many unscrupulous people were exploiting the farmers. These people would approach the farmers and tell them that they were sent by the government to get rid of snakes in their fields. The poor farmers believed them and allowed these people to catch the Rat Snakes, cobras and water snakes. The farmers were happy to get rid of the snakes. When we went to such places and told them that the snakes were In fact, the farmer's friend they were not ready to believe. We explained to them as to how the snakes kept the rat population in check and thereby protected the yield of the farmer. We briefly told them how a single pair of rats could become thousands if left to breed without any checks. Nature had a way of control through the snakes. The rats, apart from eating the rice, wheat and other produce, would also contaminate the food with their excreta and make it unfit for consumption. Moreover, the danger posed by the possibility of diseases transmitted by rats was far more than the possibility of fatal snake bites.

The response in all the villages we visited was the same and spontaneous. All of them, in one voice, told us that henceforth, they would not allow anybody to come to their fields and exploit them with false assurances and cause ecological damage by capturing snakes for the illegal snake skin trade.

We had to submit a report to the government regarding the outcome of the program. We were very happy to mention that this change was brought about in a small number of villages through this effort.

In conclusion, I would like to tell the readers that at present the Trust does not have any animals under its care. From the last several years the Trust is involved only in giving education and advice to people regarding problems concerning animals.

WHAT ARE THESE?

1. Cotton mouth
2. Diamond back
3. Tic Polonga
4. Massasauga
5. Mussurana
6. Copper head
7. Fer de lance
8. Boomslang
9. Bronze back
10. Sidewinder
11. Bush master
12. Urutu
13. Ringhal
14. Taipan
15. Jararaca
16. Jararacusu
17. Matamata
18. Frog mouth
19. Cus cus
20. Aye aye
21. Kookaburra
22. Hell bender
23. Urubu
24. Fordonia

For answers see next page

1. Cotton mouth is a pit viper. Also called water moccasin.

2. Diamond back is a rattle snake.

3. Tic polonga is also called Russell's Viper.

4. Massasuaga is a rattle snake.

5. Mussurana is a non-poisonous snake, specialising in eating other snakes by constricting the prey.

6. Copperhead is a pit viper.

7. Fer de lance is also a pit viper

8. Boomslang is a big venomous snake with poison in rear fangs.

9. Bronze back is a harmless tree dwelling snake.

10. Side winder is a horned rattle snake.

11. Bush master is the longest pit viper.

12. Urutu is a pit viper from South America.

13. Ringhal is a spitting cobra.

14. Taipan is one of the most poisonous snakes in Australia.

15. Jararaca is a pit viper native to Brazil.

16. Jararacusu is also a pit viper from South America.

17. Matamata is fresh water turtle in South America.

18. Frog mouth is also called as the Night Jar and is a nocturnal bird.

19. Cus cus is common name for an Australian marsupial. Females have a pouch like the kangaroo.

20. Aye aye is a lemur from Madagascar with a long middle finger to poke into holes in trees to ferret out insects.

21. Kookaburra is a terrestrial king fisher bird of Australia.

22. Hellbender is the largest aquatic salamander in America.

23. Urubu is a black vulture.

24. Fordonia is a crab eating aquatic snake.

QR CODES

Sheeba's routine at home

Sheeba after relocation

Barn owl chick being fed

Fruit bat drinking milk

Pangolin the scaly ant-eater

Parakeet playing with pencil

For more such videos, please visit the channel Mini Zoo on YouTube

www.ingramcontent.com/pod-product-compliance
Lightning Source LLC
Chambersburg PA
CBHW051058250726
48656CB00001B/349